Prejudicial Appearances

Prejudicial Appearances

The Logic of American Antidiscrimination Law

Robert C. Post, with K. Anthony Appiah,

Judith Butler, Thomas C. Grey, and Reva B. Siegel

Duke University Press | Durham and London 2001

© 2001 Duke University Press

All of the essays in this book originally appeared in
volume 88 of the *California Law Review* (January 2000),
and are © California Law Review, Inc.   All rights reserved
Printed in the United States of America on acid-free paper ∞
Typeset in Adobe Minion by Tseng Information Systems, Inc.
Library of Congress Cataloging-in-Publication Data
appear on the last printed page of this book.

Contents

Robert C. Post | Prejudicial Appearances:
The Logic of American Antidiscrimination Law   1

K. Anthony Appiah | Stereotypes and the Shaping of Identity   55

Judith Butler | "Appearances Aside"   73

Thomas C. Grey | Cover Blindness   85

Reva B. Siegel | Discrimination in the Eyes of the
Law: How "Color Blindness" Discourse Disrupts
and Rationalizes Social Stratification   99

Robert C. Post | Response to Commentators   153

Contributors   165

Index   167

Prejudicial Appearances

Robert C. Post | Prejudicial Appearances:

The Logic of American Antidiscrimination Law

There is a logic to the structure of American antidiscrimination law. This logic is apparent in the official opinions of judges and administrative agencies, in the expert commentary of scholars, and in the visions of the popular imagination. The influence of this logic extends from the drafting of the most modest city ordinances to the interpretation of the federal Constitution itself. It is a logic that expresses the essential principles of post–World War II American liberalism, which stress both the inherent dignity of each individual and the need for a rational and efficient economy.

To challenge this logic is to confront the pervasive and unconscious power of common sense. But it is nevertheless a challenge that I shall pursue in this essay. I shall argue that the sway of this logic has caused courts seriously to misapprehend the actual operation of American antidiscrimination law. It has led judges to craft legal rules as though antidiscrimination law could liberate individuals from the thrall of social "stereotypes," when in fact that law can intervene instead only to reshape the nature and content of social stereotypes. It has led judges to equate instrumentally rational employment rules with non-discriminatory employment rules, when in fact rationally functional standards can and do perpetuate discrimination. The contemporary logic of American antidiscrimination law has also contributed to the development of arbitrary and inarticulate doctrine. It has sustained a deep insensitivity to entrenched social inequalities, and it has underwritten an unfortunate demonization of affirmative action.

These are large claims, claims belied by the pride most of us justifiably feel in the revolution in gender and racial relations propelled by antidiscrimination law during the past thirty-five years. These genuine accomplishments constitute the common sense of contemporary antidiscrimination law. To perceive the limits of that common sense, therefore, we shall have to step outside the well-known contexts of race and gender. We shall have to examine how the logic of antidiscrimination law functions when applied in unfamiliar circumstances.

To most Americans, Santa Cruz in January 1992 would represent quite alien territory. At that time the Santa Cruz City Council proposed an ordinance that would prohibit discrimination against persons on the basis of "personal appearance."[1] First advanced by a group called the Body Image Task Force, the proposed law quickly became known in the media as "the 'purple hair ordinance' or the 'ugly ordinance.'"[2] It provoked an intense and raucous[3] controversy about the merits of what was called anti-lookism.[4]

Anti-lookism cuts deeply into the social fabric. Social relationships characteristically transpire through the medium of appearances; an ability to interpret the many meanings conveyed by appearances is required for fluency in the language of social life. Balzac, for example, once observed that the "mind of a man could be ascertained by the manner in which he holds his cane."[5] Because such judgments are the

1. David Ratner, "Santa Cruz Gives Tentative OK to Law on Personal Appearance," *S.F. Chron.*, Jan. 15, 1992, at A1.
2. Wendy Brown, *States of Injury: Power and Freedom in Late Modernity* 65–66 (1995).
3. *See* "California in Brief; Santa Cruz; Council Backs Ban on Looks Bias," *L.A. Times*, Feb. 13, 1992, at B8.
4. Editorial, "Santa Cruz' Weirdocracy," *Wash. Times*, Jan. 21, 1992, at F2.
5. "L'esprit d'un homme se devine à la manière dont il porte sa canne." Honoré de Balzac, *Traité de La Vie Élégante* 35 (1922).

stuff of ordinary life, Oscar Wilde famously quipped that "it is only shallow people who do not judge by appearances. The true mystery of the world is the visible, not the invisible." [6] The presentation of appearances in everyday life is not merely a matter of the external surfaces of the self, for appearances are also connected to identity. A postmodern sensibility would be tempted to press this point very far, as, for example, does Susan Sontag when she observes that "our manner of appearing is our manner of being. The mask is the face." [7]

The draft Santa Cruz ordinance proposed to render appearances invisible. It would do so not merely in the context of the state's treatment of its citizens, but also in the context of ordinary employment and housing transactions among private persons. It is no wonder, then, that the ordinance prompted cries of outrage. "If someone has 14 earrings in their ears and their nose—and who knows where else—and spiky green hair and smells like a skunk," commented Kathy Manoff, owner of a small restaurant, "I don't know why I have to hire them." [8] Newspaper editorials scorned the ordinance as extending "the power of the state over private judgments that are perfectly normal discriminatory responses to human eccentricities." [9] Columnist Joseph Farah wondered, "Let's say you're a newspaper editor looking for someone to cover the police beat. An experienced professional journalist wants the job, but he shows up for the interview wearing a dress. Does he get a chance to be our ace crime reporter?" [10]

Supporters of the proposed ordinance, however, insisted that it

---

6. Oscar Wilde, *The Picture of Dorian Gray* 22 (Isobel Murray ed., Oxford 1981) (1891).
7. Susan Sontag, *Against Interpretation* 18 (Delta 1981) (1965); *see also* Judith Butler, *Gender Trouble: Feminism and the Subversion of Identity* 141 (1990): "If gender attributes . . . are not expressive but performative, then these attributes effectively constitute the identity they are said to express or reveal. . . . If gender attributes and acts, the various ways in which a body shows or produces its cultural signification, are performative, then there is no preexisting identity by which an act or attribute might be measured."
8. Richard C. Paddock, "California Album; Santa Cruz Grants Anti-Bias Protection to the Ugly," *L.A. Times,* May 25, 1992, at A3.
9. "Santa Cruz' Weirdocracy," *supra* note 4.
10. Joseph Farah, "Job Bias Law Is Stretched to Cover the Ugly," *L.A. Times,* Feb. 7, 1992, at B7.

merely forbade superficial judgments based on "stereotypes."[11] They argued that because the real worth of persons did not inhere in their external appearance, important decisions regarding employment and housing ought not to depend on such an irrelevant characteristic, particularly when decisions based on appearance so often merely express "simple bigotry."[12] The efforts of employers to "control the look of their workforce" were said to "smack of the kind of mentality that kept blacks and other minorities out of the public eye for years until civil rights protections were enacted."[13]

When carefully parsed, proponents of the proposed Santa Cruz ordinance made (at least) three distinct kinds of claims. The first concerns equality. Blinding employers and landlords to appearance was seen by some as a way of making everyone equal in that regard. Thus Smiley Rogers, "a sales clerk at Bead It, a popular bead store, who ha[d] a full beard, tie[d] his long hair in a ponytail and sport[ed] a button" reading "Proudly Serving My Corporate Masters," expressed his "love" for the ordinance because "it gets everyone down to an equal level."[14]

11. David Ratner, "Appearance Law Faces 2nd Vote in Santa Cruz," *S.F. Chron.*, Jan. 16, 1992, at A15.

12. Martha Groves, "Looks Won't Mean a Lot if Anti-Bias Law Is Approved," *L.A. Times*, Jan. 24, 1992, at A3 (quoting Dawn Atkins, an anthropologist and member of the Body Image Task Force). One reporter quoted Sara Leonard, "who prefers to be called Sara Hell," concerning the misleading nature of external appearances. "Hell said she had been turned away from restaurants and jobs because of the combined effect of her black leather, dangling skeleton earring and long lock of fuchsia hair on an otherwise shaved head. The tattoo has not helped. She said that despite her bachelor's degree, she has had a hard time finding work. 'Because I have a tattoo on my head, I'm treated like a cretin,' she said." Katherine Bishop, "Santa Cruz Journal; With a Résumé in Hand and a Ring in the Nose," *N.Y. Times*, Feb. 13, 1992, at A18.

13. Stephen G. Hirsch, "Santa Cruz Law Could Be Attacked for Vagueness; Proposed Ordinance Would Bar Bias Based on Appearance," *The Recorder*, Jan. 17, 1992, at 1 (referring to the views of ACLU attorney Matthew Coles). Opponents of the ordinance particularly resented this characterization, arguing that "the focus of expanding and securing rights ought to be placed on those conditions truly irrelevant to a person's character and ability, such as race. But this puts hair color and skin color on the same moral plane." James Lileks, "Equality for the, uh, Different," *Minneapolis Star Trib.*, Jan. 19, 1992, at 25A.

14. Paddock, *supra* note 8.

The logic of effacing appearance to achieve equality is explored in Kurt Vonnegut's short story "Harrison Bergeron," which begins:

The year was 2081, and everybody was finally equal. They weren't only equal before God and the law. They were equal every which way. Nobody was smarter than anybody else. Nobody was better looking than anybody else. Nobody was stronger or quicker than anybody else. All this equality was due to the 211th, 212th, and 213th Amendments to the Constitution, and to the unceasing vigilance of agents of the United States Handicapper General.[15]

Vonnegut postulates a world in which government officials make everyone equal in every respect: Those who are graceful must wear weights; those who are smart must be distracted to reduce their intelligence to normal levels; and those who are beautiful must wear masks. The goal is to create a society that is "absolutely uncompetitive."[16]

Vonnegut envisions this world as a nightmare dystopia, in which human excellence, all that is fine and beautiful, has been brought "down to an equal level." He imagines a ballet in which the dancers are "no better than anybody else would have been. . . . They were burdened with sashweights and bags of birdshot, and their faces were masked, so that no one, seeing a free and graceful gesture or a pretty face, would feel like something the cat drug in."[17] If everything is equal, Vonnegut implies, then nothing much matters anyway.

Equality in this stringent sense was never, of course, the aim of the proposed Santa Cruz ordinance. From its earliest draft, it specifically permitted employment decisions to be based on appearance if "relevant to job performance."[18] The author of the ordinance could thus defend it on the grounds that "people should be judged on the basis of real criteria, their ability to perform the job or pay the rent, and that

15. Kurt Vonnegut Jr., "Harrison Bergeron," in *Welcome to the Monkey House* 7 (Dell Publishing 1970) (1950). For another fictional study of equality and appearance, *see* L. P. Hartley, *Facial Justice* (1960).

16. Vonnegut, *supra* note 15, at 10.

17. *Id.* at 8.

18. Ratner, *supra* note 11.

should be the sole criteria."[19] "What this ordinance is really saying," he explained, "is, hire the best-qualified person."[20] The Santa Cruz ordinance was therefore aimed not at equality but at equal opportunity, at allowing all to compete on equal terms for the title of "best-qualified person."

An alternative claim advanced by the ordinance's proponents concerns personal autonomy. A person's capacity to control the presentation of himself, through choices of hair color, tattoos, or clothing, is certainly an important form of self-expression, too precious, it was argued, to be controlled by employers or landlords.[21] One can recognize this theme in the attitude of a performance artist named Gabriel at the city council meeting considering the Santa Cruz ordinance:

preservation of self expression (handwritten margin note)

> A striking-looking woman with a partially shaved head and a thin black diagonal line drawn across her face, she said she was tired of being portrayed as an extremist.
>
> "It's regarded as a threat," she said.
>
> She rejected those who would judge her and sought to up the ante.

19. Paddock, *supra* note 8 (quoting City Councilman Neal Coonerty).
20. Groves, *supra* note 12 (quoting City Councilman Neal Coonerty).
21. This theme is quite common in the numerous constitutional cases that challenge the right of the state to set standards regulating hair length. The classic statement of the position is by no less a figure than Judge John Minor Wisdom:

> To me the right to wear one's hair as one pleases, although unspecified in our Bill of Rights, is a "fundamental" right protected by the Due Process Clause. Hair is a purely personal matter — a matter of personal style which for centuries has been one aspect of the manner in which we hold ourselves out to the rest of the world. Like other elements of costume, hair is a symbol: of elegance, of efficiency, of affinity and association, of non-conformity and rejection of traditional values. A person shorn of the freedom to vary the length and style of his hair is forced against his will to hold himself out symbolically as a person holding ideas contrary, perhaps, to ideas he holds most dear. Forced dress, including forced hair style, humiliates the unwilling complier, forces him to submerge his individuality in the "undistracting" mass, and in general smacks of the exaltation of organization over member, unit over component, and state over individual. I always thought this country does not condone such repression.

Argument for hair length (handwritten margin note)

Karr v. Schmidt, 460 F.2d 609, 621 (5th Cir. 1972) (Wisdom, J., dissenting).

Description of hair length can be associated w/ description of email handle or username. (handwritten note at bottom)

"I wish I had blue hair tonight," she said. "There's such a national fear of people having blue hair."[22]

The theme of self-expression, however, rests on the seemingly para- *using appearance to communicate* doxical notion that persons have the right both to use their appearance to communicate meanings, including messages of "threat," and simul- *then require others to ignore* taneously to require others to ignore these messages. If we concentrate on employment relationships, we can see that the self-determination of the employee must be set against the autonomy of the employer to present a particular image of her business. Employers thus quite reasonably objected to the theme of self-expression on the grounds that "if someone looks and acts as if they don't care what others think, they risk being rejected."[23]

This line of logic was apparently convincing to the drafters of the Santa Cruz ordinance, for in April 1992, they ultimately enacted an ordinance that prohibited discrimination on the basis of "physical characteristic," which was defined as "a bodily condition or bodily characteristic of any person which is from birth, accident, or disease, or from any natural physical development, or any other event outside the control of that person including individual physical mannerisms."[24] As actually passed, therefore, the Santa Cruz ordinance proscribed discrimination based only on aspects of bodily appearance that were beyond a person's control. Employers were thus free to evaluate employees based on the messages conveyed by their choice of clothes, tattoos, or artificial hair color.[25]

22. Jane Meredith Adams, "California City Faces Raging Dress Code War," *Chi. Trib.,* Feb. 16, 1992, at C4.
23. *Id.* (quoting businessman Noel Smith).
24. Santa Cruz, Cal., Mun. Code §§ 9.83.01, 9.83.02(13) (1992) ("An Ordinance of the City of Santa Cruz Adding Chapter 9.83 to the Santa Cruz Municipal Code Pertaining to the Prohibition of Discrimination").
25. The District of Columbia, it should be noted, does prohibit discrimination on the basis of "personal appearance," which it defines as "the outward appearance of any person, irrespective of sex, with regard to bodily condition or characteristics, manner or style of dress, and manner or style of personal grooming, including, but not limited to, hair style and beards." D.C. Code Ann. §§ 1-2501, 1-2502(22) (1999).

As reformulated, the Santa Cruz ordinance essentially rests on a third claim, that of fairness. Just as it is "simple bigotry" to discriminate against persons merely because of the accident of race, so it is unjust to discriminate against persons merely because of physical characteristics imposed on them by birth, accident, or disease. The case is different, however, if these characteristics are relevant to the requirements of a job. Thus, the ordinance forbids only "arbitrary discrimination . . . based on . . . physical characteristic"; that is, discrimination not required by "a bona fide occupational qualification."[26]

To capture the full force of this logic, one need only recall the wrenching letter to Nathanael West's Miss Lonelyhearts:

Dear Miss Lonelyhearts—

I am sixteen years old now and I dont know what to do and would appreciate it if you could tell me what to do. When I was a little girl it was not so bad because I got used to the kids on the block makeing fun of me, but now I would like to have boy friends like the other girls and go out on Saturday nites, but no boy will take me because I was born without a nose—although I am a good dancer and have a nice shape and my father buys me pretty clothes.

I sit and look at myself all day and cry. I have a big hole in the middle of my face that scares people even myself so I cant blame the boys for not wanting to take me out. My mother loves me, but she crys terrible when she looks at me.

What did I do to deserve such a terrible bad fate? . . . Ought I commit suicide?

Sincerely yours,

Desperate[27]

---

26. Santa Cruz, Cal., Mun. Code §§ 9.83.01, 9.83.08(6). The full list of the ordinance's prohibitions reads: "It is the intent of the city council . . . to protect and safeguard the right and opportunity of all persons to be free from all forms of arbitrary discrimination, including discrimination based on age, race, color, creed, religion, national origin, ancestry, disability, marital status, sex, gender, sexual orientation, height, weight or physical characteristic." *Id.* § 9.83.01.

27. Nathanael West, *Miss Lonelyhearts & The Day of the Locust* 170–71 (New Directions Publishing 1962) (1933).

If the law can't supply "Desperate" a boyfriend, at least it can make sure that frightened employers don't deprive her of the equal opportunity to obtain a job for which she is otherwise qualified.

One need not evoke extreme cases of grotesque disfigurement to appreciate the problem. Studies abound that attractive persons receive manifold "undeserved" benefits in life as compared to unattractive persons: Juries treat them more favorably,[28] as do teachers[29] and strangers.[30] A recent study in the *American Economic Review* demonstrated that "lookism" exerts a powerful force on the labor market, so that for both men and women "wages of people with below-average looks are lower than those of average looking workers; and there is a premium in wages for good-looking people."[31] The "wage differential between attractive and ugly people is about 10% for both sexes."[32]

Facts like these have led at least one legal article to argue that because "appearance, like race and gender, is almost always an illegitimate employment criterion . . . that . . . is frequently used to make decisions based on personal dislike or prejudicial assumptions rather than actual merit," the law should "protect people against employment discrimination on the basis of largely immutable aspects of bodily and facial appearance."[33]

When TRB of the *New Republic* read this article, he was both intrigued and troubled. He was intrigued because he recognized that "the logic is impeccable": "Appearance, like race and sex and physical handi-

28. *See* Cookie Stephan and Judy Corder Tully, "The Influence of Physical Attractiveness of a Plaintiff on the Decisions of Simulated Jurors," 101 *J. Soc. Psychol.* 149 (1977).

29. *See* Margaret M. Clifford and Elaine Walster, "The Effect of Physical Attractiveness on Teacher Expectations," 46 *Soc. Educ.* 248 (1973).

30. *See* Karen Dion *et al.,* "What Is Beautiful Is Good," 24 *J. Personality & Soc. Psychol.* 285 (1972); David W. Wilson, "Helping Behavior and Physical Attractiveness," 104 *J. Soc. Psychol.* 313 (1978). For a general discussion, *see* Gordon L. Patzer, *The Physical Attractiveness Phenomenon* (1985).

31. Daniel S. Hamermesh and Jeff E. Biddle, "Beauty and the Labor Market," 84 *Am. Econ. Rev.* 1174, 1174, 1192 (1994).

32. Robert J. Barro, "So You Want to Hire the Beautiful. Well, Why Not?," *Bus. Week,* Mar. 16, 1998, at 18.

33. Note, "Facial Discrimination: Extending Handicap Law to Employment Discrimination on the Basis of Physical Appearance," 100 *Harv. L. Rev.* 2035, 2035 (1987).

cap, is an immutable characteristic. Like these other disadvantages, an unattractive appearance usually has no connection to your ability to do the job. Therefore, discrimination on this basis is just as unfair and should be outlawed."[34] Yet TRB was also troubled by the vague sense that this impeccable logic was somehow spinning out of control. What about "prejudice on the basis of a whiny voice?" he asked. Or "what about 'grouch liberation?' "[35]

There are, of course, many reasons to be concerned about the actual operation of laws prohibiting discrimination based on appearance. If one asks about the enforcement of such laws, for example, the potential for oppressive state intrusion can come to seem quite ominous. But at root TRB was unsettled not because of these practical difficulties, but because of an inarticulate, nagging suspicion that laws prohibiting discrimination based on appearance were somehow a reductio ad absurdum of the basic logic of American antidiscrimination law. Although powerfully compelling when applied to race or gender, that same logic seemed to lose its footing when applied to appearance.

In this essay I shall pursue TRB's nagging doubt. It is my hope that this inquiry can expose important aspects of the fundamental logic of American antidiscrimination law that would not quite be visible when viewed from other, more normalized perspectives. I will explore these questions chiefly in the context of laws prohibiting discrimination in employment, which, like the Santa Cruz ordinance, apply to private persons. But I shall also refer to antidiscrimination principles as they appear in constitutional law.

Antidiscrimination law in America characteristically presents itself according to a very definite logic. It is a logic that springs from a firm sense of the social reality of prejudice. Antidiscrimination law seeks to neutralize widespread forms of prejudice that pervasively disadvantage persons based on inaccurate judgments about their worth or capacities.

The unfairness of prejudice is particularly manifest when it is di-

---

34. TRB, "The Tyranny of Beauty," 197 *New Republic*, Oct. 12, 1987, at 4.
35. *Id.*

rected against immutable traits, like race or sex. But prejudice can be unfair even if it is directed against traits that are within the control of a person. American antidiscrimination laws, for example, typically prohibit discrimination based on religion and marital status, even though neither trait is "immutable." In this regard, obesity is an interesting borderline case. It is plain that there is widespread prejudice against the obese,[36] so that obesity is a deeply stigmatizing characteristic. Antidiscrimination laws sometimes forbid discrimination based on obesity when (and only when) the characteristic is conceptualized as a disability that is beyond the control of a person;[37] sometimes they prohibit such discrimination if obesity is categorized as a disability, even if the disability is partially within the control of a person;[38] and sometimes, as in the case of the Santa Cruz ordinance, antidiscrimination laws flatly forbid discrimination based on "weight."[39] Such statutes regard prejudice against the obese as unfair even if obesity is completely within the voluntary control of a person. Although this is not the occasion to elaborate the point, I suspect that legal judgments of unfairness depend on whether a stigmatizing attribute is viewed as somehow essential or integral to a person, as is their religion.

Prejudice against a stigmatizing characteristic, such as race or sex, can manifest itself through invidious judgments of the "differential

36. See Werner J. Cahnman, "The Stigma of Obesity," 9 Soc. Q. 283 (1968); Carey Goldberg, "'People of Size' Gather to Promote Fat Acceptance: Group Celebrates Idea of Liberation," N.Y. Times, July 29, 1999, at A12. One study in the New England Journal of Medicine purported to show that similarly qualified applicants to prestigious colleges were significantly less likely to be admitted if they were obese. Helen Canning and Jean Mayer, "Obesity—Its Possible Effect on College Acceptance," 275 New Eng. J. Med. 1172 (1966).

37. See, e.g., Greene v. Union Pac. R.R., 548 F. Supp. 3, 5 (W.D. Wash. 1981); Cassista v. Community Foods, Inc., 5 Cal. 4th 1050, 1063–65 (1993); Philadelphia Elec. Co. v. Commonwealth, 448 A.2d 701, 707 (Pa. 1982).

38. See, e.g., Cook v. Rhode Island, 10 F.3d 17, 23–24 (1st Cir. 1993); State Div. of Human Rights v. Xerox Corp., 491 N.Y.S.2d 106, 110 (1985).

39. See Santa Cruz, Cal., Mun. Code §§ 9.83.01, 9.83.02(13) (1992). The state of Michigan prohibits employers from discriminating based on "religion, race, color, national origin, age, sex, height, weight, or marital status." Mich. Comp. Laws Ann. § 37.2202(1)(a) (West 1999).

worth" of persons who display the characteristic,[40] or it can manifest itself through "faulty" judgments about the capacities of such persons.[41] American antidiscrimination law understands itself as negating such prejudice by eliminating or carefully scrutinizing the use of stigmatizing characteristics as a ground for judgment. The classic constitutional formulation of this perspective is Justice White's opinion for the Court in *Cleburne v. Cleburne Living Center, Inc.*,[42] in which he writes that statutory classifications of "race, alienage, or national origin"

> are so seldom relevant to the achievement of any legitimate state interest that laws grounded in such considerations are deemed to reflect prejudice and antipathy—a view that those in the burdened class are not as worthy or deserving as others. For these reasons and because such discrimination is unlikely to be soon rectified by legislative means, these laws are subject to strict scrutiny and will be sustained only if they are suitably tailored to serve a compelling state interest.
>
> Legislative classifications based on gender also call for a heightened standard of review. That factor generally provides no sensible ground for differential treatment. "What differentiates sex from such nonsuspect statuses as intelligence or physical disability . . . is that the sex characteristic frequently bears no relation to ability to perform or contribute to society." . . . Rather than resting on meaningful considerations, statutes distributing benefits and burdens between the sexes in different ways very likely reflect outmoded notions of the relative capabilities of men and women. A gender classification fails unless it is substantially related to a sufficiently important governmental interest.[43]

Judicial interpretation of Title VII, which is the portion of the Federal Civil Rights Act of 1964 that prohibits employment discrimination

40. Paul Brest, "The Supreme Court, 1975 Term—Foreword: In Defense of the Antidiscrimination Principle," 90 *Harv. L. Rev.* 1, 7 (1976).
41. Gordon W. Allport, *The Nature of Prejudice* 9 (1954).
42. 473 U.S. 432 (1985).
43. *Id.* at 440–41 (citation omitted).

on the basis of "race, color, religion, sex, or national origin,"[44] displays a similar orientation. "In passing Title VII," the Court has said, "Congress made the simple but momentous announcement that sex, race, religion, and national origin are not relevant to the selection, evaluation, or compensation of employees."[45] The point of rendering such factors irrelevant is to "target" and eliminate "stubborn but irrational prejudice."[46] In the words of one federal district court: "In our society we too often form opinions of people on the basis of skin color, religion, national origin, . . . and other superficial features. That tendency to stereotype people is at the root of some of the social ills that afflict the country, and in adopting the Civil Rights Act of 1964, Congress intended to attack these stereotyped characterizations so that people would be judged by their intrinsic worth."[47]

State antidiscrimination statutes are typically interpreted in a similar manner. Thus, the Michigan Supreme Court has observed that "civil rights acts seek to prevent discrimination against a person because of stereotyped impressions about the characteristics of a class to which the person belongs. The Michigan civil rights act is aimed at 'the prejudices and biases' borne against persons because of their membership in a certain class . . . and seeks to eliminate the effects of offensive or demeaning stereotypes, prejudices or biases."[48] The Michigan Court of Appeals has noted that "civil rights legislation has traditionally been enacted to enable individuals to have access to opportunity based upon individual merit and qualifications and to prohibit decisions based upon irrelevant characteristics."[49]

Taken as a whole, American antidiscrimination law thus follows a

---

44. Civil Rights Act of 1964 § 703(a), 78 Stat. 255 (codified as amended at 42 U.S.C. § 2000e-2(a)).

45. *Price Waterhouse v. Hopkins*, 490 U.S. 228, 239 (1989) (Brennan, J., plurality opinion). Hence, Title VII's proscription of discrimination based on sex has been taken to mean that employers are forbidden from taking "gender into account in making employment decisions. . . . [G]ender must be irrelevant to employment decisions." *Id.* at 239–40.

46. *Lam v. University of Haw.*, 40 F.3d 1551, 1563 (9th Cir. 1994).

47. *Donohue v. Shoe Corp. of Am.*, 337 F. Supp. 1357, 1359 (C.D. Cal. 1972).

48. *Miller v. C.A. Muer Corp.*, 362 N.W.2d 650, 653–54 (1984) (citation omitted).

49. *Micu v. City of Warren*, 382 N.W.2d 823, 827 (1985).

simple but powerful logic. In the context of race-based discrimination, Paul Brest has authoritatively summarized this logic as an "antidiscrimination principle" that "lies at the core of most state and federal civil rights legislation" and that "disfavor[s] classifications and other decisions and practices that depend on the race . . . of the parties affected."[50] As a result, American antidiscrimination law typically requires employers, except in exceptional and discrete circumstances such as affirmative action,[51] to make decisions as if their employees did not exhibit forbidden characteristics—as if, for example, employees had no race or sex. This is what underwrites the important trope of "blindness" that "has played a dominant role in the interpretation of antidiscrimination prohibitions."[52] Blindness renders forbidden characteristics invisible; it requires employers to base their judgments instead on the deeper and more fundamental ground of "individual merit" or "intrinsic worth."

50. Brest, *supra* note 40, at 1. Brest writes: "The antidiscrimination principle fills a special need because . . . race-dependent decisions that are rational and purport to be based solely on legitimate considerations are likely in fact to rest on assumptions of the differential worth of racial groups or on the related phenomenon of racially selective sympathy and indifference." *Id.* at 7.

51. *See, e.g., United Steelworkers of Am. v. Weber,* 443 U.S. 193 (1979). Another important exception to this generalization is the line of Title VII analysis known as "disparate impact." Following this analysis, a plaintiff need only show that a facially neutral employment practice has a disproportionately adverse impact on a protected class. "Once that threshold is reached, the burden of persuasion shifts to the employer to demonstrate that the challenged practice is job-related and justifiable as a matter of business necessity. Finally, the plaintiff has an opportunity to prove that there exists an alternative practice that would serve the employer's objectives equally well but have a less severe adverse effect." Barbara J. Flagg, "Fashioning a Title VII Remedy for Transparently White Subjective Decisionmaking," 104 *Yale L. J.* 2009, 2019 (1995). Disparate impact analysis does not require any showing that employer decisions are "based on" a forbidden category, or have any discriminatory intent, and it may in fact require employers to take forbidden categories into account so as to ensure neutrality of impact.

52. Owen M. Fiss, "A Theory of Fair Employment Laws," 38 *U. Chi. L. Rev.* 235, 235 (1971). For a good discussion of the trope of blindness in representations of justice, *see* Martin Jay, "Must Justice Be Blind? The Challenge of Images to the Law," in *Law and the Image: The Authority of Art and the Aesthetics of Law* 19–35 (Costas Douzinas and Lynda Nead eds., 1999). Jay associates the blindness of justice with the abstraction of "the exchange principle." *Id.* at 29.

In essence, the logic of American antidiscrimination law requires employers to regard their employees as though they did not display socially powerful and salient attributes, because these attributes may induce irrational and prejudiced judgments. Each time the law adds another proscribed category of discrimination, it renders yet another attribute of employees invisible to their employers. In recent years, the list of such proscribed categories has greatly expanded. The Santa Cruz ordinance, for example, prohibits "arbitrary discrimination" based on "age, race, color, creed, religion, national origin, ancestry, disability, marital status, sex, gender, sexual orientation, height, weight or physical characteristic."[53]

The Santa Cruz ordinance demands that employers interact with their employees in ways that are blind to almost everything that is normally salient in everyday social life. It is not clear, however, what such blindness actually entails. We can conceive what it would mean to treat someone in a way that renders race irrelevant; we think we know (although I have my doubts) what it would mean to treat someone in a way that renders sex irrelevant; but I suspect that we have almost no idea what it would mean physically to encounter a person and nevertheless to treat him or her in a way that renders irrelevant his or her face, voice, body, and gestures.[54] In what sense does a person without an appearance remain a person?

From this perspective, ordinances precluding discrimination based on appearance are unsettling because they seem to preclude any ordinary form of human interaction. So much has been abstracted away from the employee that, with respect to the employer, the employee is transported into something like what John Rawls has called an "original position" behind a "veil of ignorance."[55] For reasons that are analogous to antidiscrimination law, Rawls, in what has perhaps become the canonical text of post–World War II American liberalism, employs the

---

53. Santa Cruz, Cal., Mun. Code §§ 9.83.01 (1992).

54. We are, however, learning something of the deep puzzles caused by encountering bodiless persons in the virtual space of the Internet. For a fascinating study, see Sherry Turkle, *Life on the Screen: Identity in the Age of the Internet* (1995).

55. John Rawls, *A Theory of Justice* 136 (1971).

veil of ignorance to strip away all "accidents of natural endowment and . . . contingencies of social circumstance."[56] The original position is precisely designed to remove what "sets men at odds and allows them to be guided by their prejudices."[57]

The original position is for Rawls primarily a heuristic device to force us to focus on the "equality between human beings as moral persons,"[58] which is to say, "as rational beings with their own ends."[59] Sometimes it is said that antidiscrimination law effaces forbidden attributes for an analogous reason, which is to force employers to recognize the "intrinsic worth" of employees.[60] But the difficulty with this account is that employers must make distinctions between employees, and "intrinsic worth" is by hypothesis equal. So American antidiscrimination law must strip away prejudicial contingencies of social circumstance for a different reason.

In fact what antidiscrimination law seeks to uncover is an apprehension of "individual merit."[61] That is why the author of the Santa Cruz ordinance understood it as forcing employers to judge employees "on the basis of real criteria," which "is their ability to perform the job."[62]

---

56. *Id.* at 15.

57. *Id.* at 19. Behind the veil of ignorance, "no one knows his place in society, his class position or social status; nor does he know his fortune in the distribution of natural assets and abilities, his intelligence and strength, and the like." *Id.* at 137.

58. *Id.* at 19.

59. *Id.* at 12.

60. *See, e.g., supra* note 47 and accompanying text; see also *Gay Rights Coalition of Georgetown Univ. Law Ctr. v. Georgetown Univ.*, 536 A.2d 1, 37 (D.C. 1987); Brest, *supra* note 40, at 8. Sometimes the cases express this idea through the notion of "inherent dignity." *See, e.g., Sargoy v. Resolution Trust Corp.*, 8 Cal. App. 4th 1039, 1045 (1992); *Starkman v. Mann Theatres Corp.*, 227 Cal. App. 3d 1491, 1500 (1991); *Nelson v. Miwa*, 546 P.2d 1005, 1009 (Haw. 1976). For a good statement of this theme in Canadian antidiscrimination law, see the remarkable case of *Vriend v. Alberta*, No. 25285, 1998 Can. Sup. Ct. LEXIS 19, at *26 (Can. Sup. Ct. Apr. 2, 1998).

61. *See, e.g., United States v. Burke*, 504 U.S. 229, 247 (1992) (Souter, J., concurring); *Regents of the Univ. of Cal. v. Bakke*, 438 U.S. 265, 361 (1978) (Brennan, White, Marshall, and Blackmun, JJ., joint opinion); *Mardell v. Harleysville Life Ins. Co.*, 31 F.3d 1221, 1234 (3d Cir. 1994); *Martini v. Federal Nat'l Mortgage Ass'n*, 977 F. Supp. 464, 479 (D.D.C. 1997); *supra* note 49 and accompanying text.

62. *See supra* note 19.

American antidiscrimination law pushes employers toward functional justifications for their actions. In the area of Title VII law known as disparate treatment, for example, employers' reasons for particular decisions disadvantaging employees are scrutinized to determine whether they are a "pretext for the sort of discrimination prohibited" by the statute.[63] In such circumstances, employers have strong incentives to articulate "legitimate reasons" for their decisions, and these reasons are characteristically connected to the achievement of a proper "business goal."[64]

Employers must provide 'functional justifications' for actions — must be connected to achievement of a business goal.

In the area of Title VII law known as disparate impact, in which facially neutral selection procedures that have disproportionally adverse impacts on protected groups are assessed for bias, the law permits employers to defend procedures by demonstrating that they "are demonstrably a reasonable measure of job performance." "Congress has not commanded that the less qualified be preferred over the better qualified simply because of minority origins. Far from disparaging job qualifications as such, Congress has made such qualifications the controlling factor, so that race, religion, nationality, and sex become irrelevant. What Congress has commanded is that any tests used must measure the person for the job and not the person in the abstract."[65]

In the area of Title VII law known as "bona fide occupational qualification" (BFOQ), in which certain forms of overt discrimination based on sex or national origin can be justified, the Court has held that the test is whether the proposed BFOQ relates "to the 'essence' . . . or to the 'central mission of the employer's business.' "[66] Within the area of fed-

63. *McDonnell Douglas Corp. v. Green*, 411 U.S. 792, 804 (1973).

64. *Furnco Constr. Corp. v. Waters*, 438 U.S. 567, 577 (1978). Of course, as a matter of technical law, "Title VII does not make unexplained differences in treatment per se illegal nor does it make inconsistent or irrational employment practices illegal. It prohibits only intentional discrimination based upon an employee's protected class characteristics." *EEOC v. Flasher Co.*, 986 F.2d 1312, 1319 (10th Cir. 1992). I mean to imply only that Title VII pushes very hard in the direction of forcing employers to explain their decisions in light of rational business considerations, as these will prove to be the most plausible and convincing defenses to charges of discriminatory animus.

65. *Griggs v. Duke Power*, 401 U.S. 424, 436 (1971).

66. *International Union, United Auto., Aerospace and Agric. Implement Workers of Am. v.*

eral constitutional law, state classifications based on race are acceptable only if they are "justified by a compelling governmental interest and ... 'necessary to the accomplishment' of their legitimate purpose."[67]

Functional rationality, whether assessed by stricter or more deferential tests, is thus broadly regarded by American antidiscrimination law as a justification for employer decisions. The longer the list of attributes excluded by antidiscrimination law from employer consideration, the more perfectly the law pushes employers toward considerations of pure instrumental reason. From this perspective, employees can come to be seen merely as means for accomplishing the managerial purposes of an employer's business.[68] For this reason, John Schaar has criticized the equality of opportunity celebrated by antidiscrimination laws as resting on a conception of the person that reduces him or her "to a bundle of abilities, an instrument valued according to its capacity for performing socially valued functions with more or less efficiency."[69]

The image that most perfectly captures this thrust of antidiscrimination law is that of the orchestra audition. Since the 1970s American orchestras have, to overcome ingrained sex discrimination, auditioned musicians by requiring them to play behind opaque screens. Sometimes orchestras use rugs "to muffle the sound of footsteps that could betray the sex of the candidate," or sometimes a "personnel manager may ask a woman to take off her shoes and he provides the 'compensating footsteps.'"[70] In this way, the race, color, religion, sex, national origin,

orchestra Audition
-play behind A screen
-can't tell sex.

Johnson Controls, Inc., 499 U.S. 187, 203 (1991) [hereinafter "*Automobile Workers v. Johnson Controls, Inc.*"] (quoting *Dothard v. Rawlinson,* 433 U.S. 321, 333 [1977], and *Western Airlines v. Criswell,* 472 U.S. 400, 413 [1985]).

67. *Palmore v. Sidoti,* 466 U.S. 429, 432–33 (1984) (quoting *McLaughlin v. Florida,* 379 U.S. 184, 196 [1964]).

68. It is interesting to note in this regard that Rawls explicitly argues that "the concept of rationality" appropriate to the original position "must be interpreted as far as possible in the narrow sense, standard in economic theory, of taking the most effective means to given ends." Rawls, *supra* note 55, at 14.

69. John H. Schaar, "Equality of Opportunity and Beyond," in *Legitimacy in the Modern State* 193, 203 (1981).

70. Claudia Goldin and Cecilia Rouse, "Orchestrating Impartiality: The Impact of 'Blind' Auditions on Female Musicians" 8 & n.19 (National Bureau of Econ. Research

and appearance of the musician is completely masked behind a veil of ignorance, so that employment decisions are made almost entirely[71] on the basis of the pure production of sound. The musician becomes a perfectly disembodied instrument.

The image of the orchestra audition distills the logic of American antidiscrimination law. Four aspects of that logic require emphasis. First, it is no small irony that American antidiscrimination law, which springs from the noble liberal impulse to protect persons from the indignities of prejudicial mistreatment, should in the end unfold itself according to a logic that points unmistakably toward the instrumentalization of persons. If liberalism seeks to attribute equal dignity to all persons on the basis of a presocial and "universal human potential,"[72] American antidiscrimination law, in the context of employment, strangely imagines itself as transmuting persons at the very moment of their social manifestation into the object of Weberian rationalization.

Second, the audition screen is understood to counteract sex discrimination because it is assumed that musicianship is not intrinsically connected to gender. We use the screen because we believe that how persons make music does not depend on their sex; some women and some men are good musicians, and some are not. The screen permits us to focus on the pure trait of musicianship, without the distraction of gender. In Europe, where "blind auditions are still anathema," this assumption is disputed; it is claimed "that women change an orchestra's 'morale' and its 'sound.'"[73] Our own use of the screen thus re-

---

Working Paper No. 5903, 1997); *see also* "American Orchestras: All Ears," *The Economist*, Nov. 30, 1996, at 89.

71. The screen is typically removed "in the final round," so that the conductor can observe "bad playing habits." See "American Orchestras: All Ears," *supra* note 70, at 90.

72. Charles Taylor, "The Politics of Recognition," in Charles Taylor et al., *Multiculturalism: Examining the Politics of Recognition* 41 (Amy Gutmann ed., 1994).

73. "American Orchestras: All Ears," *supra* note 70, at 90. Before simply discounting European sensibilities in this matter, we should recall the "perennial question" in the United States of whether the race of a jazz musician affects the quality of his music. *See, e.g.,* Henry Louis Gates Jr., " 'Authenticity,' or the Lesson of Little Tree," *N.Y. Times Book Rev.,* Nov. 24, 1991, at 1.

Does finding out The musician is white affect your appreciation of the jazz song?

flects a particular historical understanding of the relationship between job performance and gender. We tend to presume that instrumental action is, in Habermas's phrase, "context-free,"[74] so that successful job performance is conceptualized within antidiscrimination law as logically and practically distinct from potentially stigmatizing characteristics, like sex or race. These characteristics are figured as superficial and as fundamentally disconnected from achievement; social arrangements that are instrumentally rational are concomitantly seen as nondiscriminatory.[75]

Third, the logic of invisibility exemplified by the audition screen can have powerful and constructive consequences. Use of the audition screen vastly increased the number of female musicians in American orchestras.[76] Antidiscrimination law understands itself as transformative, as fundamentally altering existing social arrangements.[77] But this project requires us imaginatively to project ourselves into alternative social circumstances. Blindness, whether enforced by a screen or by the law, can be useful and effective in this regard.

Fourth, the audition screen itself is an essentially artificial device, serviceable only in discrete, bounded, and exceptional circumstances. It cannot be generalized. Once hired, a musician must step from behind

74. Jürgen Habermas, *Toward a Rational Society: Student Protest, Science, and Politics* 93 (Jeremy J. Shapiro trans., 1970).

75. The tendency of instrumental rationality to cut across and efface the social field is evident in disparate impact analysis under Title VII. Although disparate impact analysis does not participate in the trope of blindness that characterizes so much of American antidiscrimination law, it nevertheless clearly holds that employment practices that can be instrumentally justified do not constitute discrimination, whatever the social impact of these practices on minorities or women. The question is why instrumental justification seems automatically to render social impact irrelevant. For a discussion, *see supra* notes 51 and 65 *infra* text accompanying notes 97–99.

76. See Goldin and Rouse, *supra* note 70, at 23. In Detroit, however, controversy arose about the use of the screen because the Detroit Symphony Orchestra "felt constrained in its efforts to include more African American musicians." "Sex Discrimination: Economists Find Switch to Blind Auditions Boosted Women's Ranks in Major Orchestras," *Daily Lab. Rep.*, July 15, 1997, at A-2.

77. On the transformative thrust of antidiscrimination law, see Andrew Koppelman, *Antidiscrimination Law and Social Equality* 4–10 (1996).

the screen, disclose her body and her gender, and live her professional life in the full glare of social visibility. At that point, her protection from prejudice in the conditions of her employment will lie in the logic of willful blindness legally imposed by antidiscrimination law.

[handwritten margin notes: The screen is eventually exposed as Artifice since person eventually has to step out from behind it. Also, a screen Auditions can't be held everywhere]

The law, of course, is a practical, ramshackle institution, full of compromise and contradiction. It nowhere expresses as purely as I have just done the logic of fairness and equal opportunity. Yet I strongly suspect that if one were to ask those who participate in the development and application of antidiscrimination law to explain the thrust of their enterprise, something very close to the story I have sketched will emerge, whether the interlocutor is a local councilperson drafting a town ordinance or a federal judge interpreting constitutive statutes like Title VII.

I shall call this story the "dominant conception" of American antidiscrimination law. My hypothesis is that the dominant conception distorts and masks the actual operation of antidiscrimination law and, by so doing, potentially undermines the law's coherence and usefulness as a tool of transformative social policy.

To see why this is so, we need to remind ourselves that in everyday life persons mostly inhabit neither the abstractions of an original position nor the "context-free" objectification of perfect functionality. They live instead in a social world that springs from history and that creates identities founded on contingent facts of socialization and culture.[78] American antidiscrimination law singles out for special scrutiny specific categories such as race, gender, or appearance precisely because in our world these categories are socially salient and meaningful. We treat people differently depending on whether they are men or women, black or white, beautiful or ugly. We do so because we have been socialized into a culture in which these differences matter, and matter in systematic ways. We might for the moment think of these systematic

---

78. For a discussion of the relationship between identity and contingent facts of socialization and social structure, *see* Robert Post, *Constitutional Domains* 3–15, 51–67 (1995).

differences as social practices or norms within which categories like race, gender, and beauty acquire their significance.[79]

The law is itself a social institution. It does not spring autochthonously from an "original position" or from the discipline of instrumental reason. Law is made by the very persons who participate in the social practices that constitute race, gender, and beauty. It would be astonishing, therefore, if American antidiscrimination law could transcend these categories, if it could operate in a way that rendered them truly irrelevant.[80] Yet that is exactly what the dominant conception asks us to believe.

A much more plausible picture is that antidiscrimination law is itself a social practice, which regulates other social practices, because the latter have become for one reason or another controversial. It is because the meaning of categories like race, gender, and beauty have become contested that we seek to use antidiscrimination law to reshape them in ways that reflect the purposes of the law. We might summarize this perspective by observing that antidiscrimination law always begins and ends in history, which means that it must participate in the very practices that it seeks to alter and to regulate.[81]

In the next part of this essay, I shall illustrate this conclusion by discussing the example of Title VII's prohibition against discrimination on the basis of sex. I choose this example because the subject is especially rich and because gender conventions often turn so crucially on matters of appearance.[82] In the fifth and penultimate part of this essay, I will say a few words about the practical implications of thinking about antidis-

79. For an unforgettable historical description of the nature of the "structure" of such practices, *see* Don Herzog, *Poisoning the Minds of the Lower Orders* 244–323, 326–27 (1998).

80. *See* Roderick M. Hills Jr., "You Say You Want a Revolution? The Case against the Transformation of Culture through Antidiscrimination Laws," 95 *Mich. L. Rev.* 1588, 1591 (1997).

81. *See* Reva Siegel, "Why Equal Protection No Longer Protects: The Evolving Forms of Status-Enforcing State Action," 49 *Stan. L. Rev.* 1111 (1997).

82. On the question of gender and appearance, *see* Deborah L. Rhode, *Speaking of Sex: The Denial of Gender Inequality* 15–16 (1997).

crimination law in this way, as distinct from the logic of the dominant conception.

Title VII forbids employment decisions that "discriminate against any individual . . . because of such individual's . . . sex,"[83] and it also "prohibits sex-based classifications in terms and conditions of employment . . . that adversely affect an employee's status."[84] This language is quite sweeping, and it is often said that the object of Title VII is "to strike at the entire spectrum of disparate treatment of men and women resulting from sex stereotypes."[85] Although the notion of "sex stereotypes" is never defined, it seems to refer to conventional understandings or generalizations about differences between men and women. Title VII's prohibition of sex stereotypes has been interpreted to include "both real and fictional differences between women and men."[86] Thus, for purposes of Title VII, "even a true generalization about" sex differences "is an insufficient reason for disqualifying an individual to whom the generalization does not apply."[87]

83. 42 U.S.C. § 2000e-2(a)(1) (1998).

84. *Automobile Workers v. Johnson Controls, Inc.,* 499 U.S. 187, 197 (1991). The statute reads:

> It shall be an unlawful employment practice for an employer:
>
> (1) to fail or refuse to hire or to discharge any individual, or otherwise to discriminate against any individual with respect to his compensation, terms, conditions, or privileges of employment, because of such individual's race, color, religion, sex, or national origin; or
>
> (2) to limit, segregate, or classify his employees or applicants for employment in any way which would deprive or tend to deprive any individual of employment opportunities or otherwise adversely affect his status as an employee, because of such individual's race, color, religion, sex, or national origin.

42 U.S.C. § 2000e-2(a).

85. *County of Washington v. Gunther,* 452 U.S. 161, 180 (1981) (quoting *City of Los Angeles Dep't of Water & Power v. Manhart,* 435 U.S. 702, 707 n.13 [1978]) (quoting *Sprogis v. United Air Lines, Inc.,* 444 F.2d 1194, 1198 [7th Cir. 1971]). "The Court has . . . held that employment action governed by gender stereotypes violates Title VII." Note, "The Supreme Court: Leading Cases," 112 *Harv. L. Rev.* 122, 333 (1998).

86. *Manhart,* 435 U.S. at 707.

87. *Id.* at 708.

"Generalizations" and "stereotypes" of this kind are, of course, the conventions that underwrite the social practice of gender. To eliminate all such generalizations and stereotypes would be to eliminate the practice. This ambition reflects the goal of the dominant conception, which is to disestablish the category of sex and to replace it with the imperatives of functional rationality.[88] Title VII recognizes these imperatives by providing that an employer may "discriminate on the basis"[89] of sex only "in those certain instances where . . . sex . . . is a bona fide occupational qualification [BFOQ] reasonably necessary to the normal operation of that particular business or enterprise."[90]

It was quickly recognized that the BFOQ exception had to be "interpreted narrowly"[91] or the transformative thrust of Title VII would be entirely blunted. This was accomplished by rejecting BFOQ exemptions in cases where the functional requirements of a job demanded capacities that could be conceptualized as only contingently related to sex, which is to say as statistically distributed between the sexes. The paradigmatic example is the refusal to grant a BFOQ exemption to an employer who claims that women should not be hired for particular positions because "the arduous nature of the work-related activity renders women physically unsuited for the jobs."[92] Because strength can

88. Title VII has been interpreted "to mean that gender must be irrelevant to employment decisions." *Price Waterhouse v. Hopkins,* 490 U.S. 228, 240 (1989) (Brennan, J., plurality opinion). "When an employer ignored the attributes enumerated in the statute, Congress hoped, it naturally would focus on the qualifications of the applicant or employee. The intent to drive employers to focus on qualifications rather than on race, religion, sex, or national origin is the theme of a good deal of the statute's legislative history." *Id.* at 243.

89. *Automobile Workers v. Johnson Controls, Inc.,* 499 U.S. 187, 200 (1991).

90. 42 U.S.C. § 2000e-2(e)(1). The statute reads: "Notwithstanding any other provision of this subchapter, (1) it shall not be an unlawful employment practice for an employer to hire and employ employees . . . on the basis of his religion, sex, or national origin in those certain instances where religion, sex, or national origin is a bona fide occupational qualification reasonably necessary to the normal operation of that particular business or enterprise."

91. 29 C.F.R. § 1604.2(a) (1998).

92. *Rosenfeld v. Southern Pac. Co.,* 444 F.2d 1219, 1223 (9th Cir. 1971). The court offered as an example of a legal BFOQ the hiring of a woman "for the position of a wet-nurse." *Id.* at 1224.

be seen to be statistically distributed between the sexes, so that some women and some men have strength and some do not, courts hold that such a classification by sex constitutes unlawful discrimination. They explain that the purpose of Title VII is "to eliminate subjective assumptions and traditional stereotyped conceptions regarding the physical ability of women to do particular work"; it is therefore a violation of Title VII "if a male employee may be appointed to a particular position on a showing that he is physically qualified, but a female employee is denied an opportunity to demonstrate personal physical qualification."[93]

This perspective marks a significant alteration of traditional gender roles. It essentially severs the connection between certain kinds of capacities and sex, and it constructs a special kind of legal subject, which is the bearer of these capacities and as to which sex is irrelevant.[94] This legal subject is the "individual," who is seen as the beneficiary of the equal opportunity promised by Title VII. "The statute's focus on the individual is unambiguous. It precludes treatment of individuals as simply components of a racial, religious, sexual or national class."[95] EEOC regulations provide that "the principle of nondiscrimination requires that individuals be considered on the basis of individual capacities and not on the basis of any characteristics generally attributed to the group."[96]

Under the influence of the dominant conception, courts have interpreted the statutory focus on "individuals" as requiring the creation of legal subjects whose capacities bypass gender conventions and attach directly to the "context-free" logic of instrumental reason. Judicial

---

93. *Id.* at 1225. EEOC regulations provide that a BFOQ exception should not be granted where "the refusal to hire an individual" is "based on stereotyped characterizations of the sexes. Such stereotypes include, for example, that men are less capable of assembling intricate equipment; that women are less capable of aggressive salesmanship." 29 C.F.R. § 1604.2(a)(1)(ii) (1998).

94. "Title VII's traditional focus has been to prohibit employer policies and practices that treat workers differently based on gender-based expectations of who men and women are supposed to be." Vicki Schultz, "Reconceptualizing Sexual Harassment," 107 *Yale L. J.* 1683, 1738 (1998).

95. *City of Los Angeles Dep't of Water & Power v. Manhart,* 435 U.S. 702, 708 (1978).

96. 29 C.F.R. § 1604.2(a)(1)(ii) (1998).

rhetoric envisions "individuals" who exist entirely outside of the historical contingencies of received gender norms. In actual life, however, persons always inhabit historical contingency; they neither originate behind a veil of ignorance, nor subsist within the asocial environment of a "context-free" functional rationality. Because of the particular facts of our history, we do not encounter in everyday interactions sexless "individuals," but rather men and women. Sex is thus pervasively important in our understanding of the capacities of persons. This is as true for those who make and apply the law as it is for those whom the law seeks to regulate. Like all legal interventions, Title VII is firmly embedded within this historical context.

It is therefore implausible to read Title VII as mandating that gender conventions be obliterated. It makes far more sense to interpret the statute as seeking to alter the particular meanings of these conventions as they are displayed in specific contexts. On this account, Title VII would in the context of employment require us to sever the connection between gender and some capacities, such as strength, but not to eliminate gender as such. In contrast to the dominant conception, this way of conceptualizing the statute would not require us to imagine a world of sexless individuals, but would instead challenge us to explore the precise ways in which Title VII should alter the norms by which sex is given social meaning. The difference between the two perspectives can be made visible by examining how Title VII deals with the question of customer preferences.

It might be said that the essential purpose of any business is to satisfy its customers and thereby to make a profit. But if customers participate in the same gender practices that Title VII seeks to modify, business decisions seeking to gratify customers will undermine the transformative thrust of Title VII. So, for example, soon after the enactment of the statute an armored car company sought to obtain a BFOQ exception for its policy of refusing to hire women courier guards on the grounds that "many of its customers would deny it business if [it] used women guards, since the customers would feel that women could not provide the degree of security needed."[97] The company's request evoked the

97. EEOC Dec. No. 70-11, EEOC Decs. (CCH) ¶ 6025 (July 8, 1969).

BFOQ
Bona Fide Occupational Qualification

ideal of functional rationality, because it argued that a BFOQ was necessary to maximize profits. Yet the request was controversial because it revealed a potentially disturbing tension between the ideal of gender blindness and functional rationality. It indicated that in a world of historically given gender conventions, functional rationality may in some circumstances actually reinforce traditional gender understandings.

We might better grasp the deep implications of the armored car company's request by returning to our image of the orchestra audition. The company's request suggests that the image may mislead us because it too quickly conflates the sex blindness created by a veil of ignorance with a purified form of instrumental rationality. The whole point of the audition screen, after all, is to remove potential prejudice that might interfere with a more accurate appreciation of the quality of a musician's performance. But if that quality were actually dependent on a musician's sex—if men in fact made better music because of their sex—then the screen would no longer serve this function. We would thus be put to a choice. Either we could continue to seek the best orchestra possible, fully knowing that this pursuit would incorporate sex-related traits, or we could sacrifice the quality of our orchestra to pursue a norm of sex equality.[98]

In effect, the request of the armored car company was for the EEOC to adopt the first option. But notice that under either option the audition screen would be rendered superfluous. Under the first option, hiring the best possible orchestra would require knowing the sex of musicians, so that the ideal of sex blindness would be trumped by the imperatives of instrumental rationality. Under the second option, the goal of hiring specific numbers of female and male musicians would trump the ideal of sex blindness in the name of sex equality. In either case, the screen would have ceased to serve a useful function.

This illustrates the profound way in which both the ideal of sex blindness and the dominant conception presuppose a certain relationship between potentially stigmatizing characteristics like sex (or race) and instrumental rationality. Sex blindness does not make sense unless

98. This latter option is essentially the holding of *City of Los Angeles Dep't of Water & Power v. Manhart*, 435 U.S. 702 (1978).

these characteristics are understood to be fundamentally disconnected from functional rationality. The coherence of the dominant conception requires us to conceptualize the trait of musicianship as statistically distributed between the sexes, like the trait of physical strength.

Not surprisingly, the EEOC firmly rejected the exception requested by the armored car company. The commission stated that the business had provided "no factual evidence, based on experience or otherwise, that would support its assertion that all or nearly all females are unfit for the position of Courier Guard."[99] The armored car company, however, had never argued that women could not perform the function of a courier guard; it had instead contended that maximizing its profits required pandering to the expectations of its customers. By focusing the question of functional rationality on the narrow issue of the job performance of courier guards, instead of on the larger issue of the success of the business, the EEOC essentially insisted that the norm of sex blindness remain firmly attached to a concept of functional rationality.

An obvious difficulty with the EEOC's proposed focus is that the constituent tasks of a business are significant only if the business is itself successful, so that the instrumental logic required for the maintenance of an armored car company would seem to take analytic and practical precedence over that required for the successful performance of the job of a courier guard. Regardless of whether one accepts this point, however, it is clear that the commission's decision renders instrumental rationality a malleable category, to be manipulated for the purpose of sustaining a correspondence between the norm of sex blindness and functional rationality. The effect of this correspondence is to foreclose inquiry into the justification, and therefore into the reach and significance, of the law's pursuit of the ideal of sex blindness.

Once functional rationality and sex blindness are analytically separated, however, this inquiry cannot be evaded. The commission's decision has come to stand for the black-letter rule that Title VII will not permit an appeal to customer preferences to render "nugatory the will of Congress"[100] that capacities conceptualized as statistically distrib-

---

99. EEOC Dec. No. 70–11, *supra* note 97, at 4048.

100. *Id.* The EEOC stated that the company's request "is, in law, without merit, since it

uted between the sexes be determined on an individualized basis.[101] The question, therefore, is which capacities are to be conceptualized by the law as "sexless" in this way. If we cannot use the logic of instrumental rationality as a guide, by what alternative rationale are such capacities to be identified?

Because the dominant conception seeks completely to suppress gender stereotypes and generalizations, it would suggest that all capacities be conceptualized as statistically distributed between the sexes. It would thus deny the legitimacy of all customer preferences that incorporate traditional gender conventions. Contemporary EEOC regulations essentially take this position,[102] which is echoed by judicial pronouncements to the effect that "stereotypic impressions of male and female roles do not qualify gender as a BFOQ." [103] Yet if judicial decisions are carefully parsed, it can be seen that such pronouncements, which

---

presumes that customers' desires may be accommodated even at the price of rendering nugatory the will of Congress." *Id.* This response is especially striking given that the EEOC could have argued, as John Hart Ely has pointed out to me, that if all armored car companies were forced to hire female guards, no particular company would be placed at a competitive disadvantage. Evidently, the EEOC was unwilling to contemplate even the possibility of a theoretical divergence between sex blindness and functional rationality.

101. *See, e.g., Diaz v. Pan Am. World Airways,* 442 F.2d 385, 389 (5th Cir. 1971), cert. denied, 404 U.S. 950 (1971): "While we recognize that the public's expectation of finding one sex in a particular role may cause some initial difficulty, it would be totally anomalous if we were to allow the preferences and prejudices of the customers to determine whether the sex discrimination was valid. Indeed, it was, to a large extent, these very prejudices the Act was meant to overcome. Thus, we feel that customer preference may be taken into account only when it is based on the company's inability to perform the primary function or service it offers."

102. *See* 29 C.F.R. § 1604.2(a) (1998):

(1) The Commission will find that the following situations do not warrant the application of the bona fide occupational qualification exception:

. . . .

(iii) The refusal to hire an individual because of the preferences of . . . customers except as covered specifically in paragraph (a)(2) of this section.

(2) Where it is necessary for the purpose of authenticity or genuineness, the Commission will consider sex to be a bona fide occupational qualification, e.g., an actor or actress.

103. *Fernandez v. Wynn Oil Co.,* 653 F.2d 1273, 1276 (9th Cir. 1981); *see also Sprogis v. United Air Lines,* 444 F.2d 1194, 1199 (7th Cir. 1971).

express the perspective of the dominant conception, do not correspond to the actual shape of the law.

Consider, in this context, the case of *Wilson v. Southwest Airlines*,[104] in which Southwest Airlines sought to defend its policy of hiring only "attractive female flight attendants" as a B F O Q because its "sexy image" was "crucial to the airline's continued financial success."[105] It is (at present) difficult to imagine a world in which sexual attraction would be regarded as a capacity borne by individuals as to whom sex is irrelevant. Put another way, sexual attraction is so firmly attached to existing gender roles that the effort to transform such roles by dislodging the "stereotypes" presently manifested by sexual attraction seems an implausible ambition for the law.

Certainly the court in *Wilson* was not about to interpret Title VII as disestablishing such fundamental gender practices. The court cleverly solved this problem by differentiating businesses whose primary purpose is to sell sexual attraction, such as Playboy Clubs,[106] from such businesses as Southwest Airlines, where the purpose of the business does not involve sexual gratification. The court conceded that where "sex appeal is itself the dominant service provided . . . customer preference for one sex only . . . would logically be so strong that the employer's ability to perform the primary function or service offered would be undermined by not hiring members of the authentic sex or group exclusively."[107] In these circumstances, sex would constitute a B F O Q.

But the court distinguished such businesses from Southwest Airlines, whose "primary function is to transport passengers safely and quickly from one point to another," rather than to sell "vicarious sex

104. 517 F. Supp 292 (N.D. Tex. 1981).

105. *Id.* at 293. Southwest was known as the "love airline." *Id.* at 294. "Unabashed allusions to love and sex pervade all aspects of Southwest's public image. Its T.V. commercials feature attractive attendants in fitted outfits, catering to male passengers while an alluring feminine voice promises in-flight love. On board, attendants in hot-pants (skirts are now optional) serve 'love bites' (toasted almonds) and 'love potions' (cocktails)." *Id.* at n.4. "Sex appeal has been used to attract male customers to the airline. . . . The evidence was undisputed that Southwest's unique, feminized image played and continues to play an important role in the airline's success." *Id.* at 295.

106. *See id.* at 301.

107. *Id.*

entertainment."[108] Having defined the purpose of Southwest Airlines in this way, the court could easily conclude that the capacities necessary to ensure safe and efficient transportation could properly be attached to individuals as to whom sex is irrelevant. In effect, the court transformed the question into a simple variant of the courier guard case.

The court in *Wilson* recognized that Title VII did not seek to alter certain gender conventions. It was unwilling to imagine a world in which sexual attraction was statistically distributed among "individuals," so that men and women would be attracted to persons regardless of their sex. But the court was nevertheless willing to intervene to shape existing practices within the airline industry. By exercising the authority to manipulate the definition of the "primary function" of the industry, the court held that sexual attraction was not a relevant capacity of flight attendants. Although this represents an important legal modification of a large industry, the court also implicitly acknowledged the limits of the law's efforts to effect such transformations.

The nature of these limits can be seen by contrasting *Wilson* with a case such as *Craft v. Metromedia, Inc.*,[109] in which a female TV news anchor alleged that different standards of "appearance" were imposed on her than on her male counterparts. The court accepted as a fact that KMBC, the employer television station, "required both male and female on-air personnel to maintain professional, businesslike appearances, 'consistent with community standards,' and that the station enforced that requirement in an evenhanded, nondiscriminatory manner."[110] The court also recognized, however, that KMBC imposed fashion requirements that were gender-specific, so that the plaintiff was instructed to "purchase more blouses with 'feminine touches,' such as bows and ruffles, because many of her clothes were 'too masculine.' "[111] The court chose to accept these requirements on the grounds that they were " 'obviously critical' to KMBC's economic well-being," given the "conservatism thought necessary in the Kansas City market."[112] In con-

108. *Id.* at 302.
109. 766 F.2d 1205, 1207 (8th Cir. 1985).
110. *Id.* at 1209–10.
111. *Id.* at 1214.
112. *Id.* at 1215.

trast to *Wilson,* the court in *Craft* refused to redefine the nature of the job qualifications at issue by recharacterizing the purposes of the business: "While we believe the record shows an overemphasis by KMBC on appearance, we are not the proper forum in which to debate the relationship between newsgathering and dissemination and considerations of appearance and presentation—i.e., questions of substance versus image—in television journalism."[113]

In *Craft,* therefore, the court declined to distinguish between the requirements of disseminating the news and the requirements of generating an audience. It consequently accepted the gender conventions implicit in customer preferences as a justification for gender-specific appearance regulations,[114] thereby sheltering these conventions from the transformative force of Title VII.[115] KMBC was authorized by the court to treat its news anchor as a woman, rather than as an individual for whom sex is irrelevant.[116] The distinction between *Wilson* and *Craft* thus marks a line in the social geography of the law's willingness to disturb existing gender roles.

The demarcations of this social geography are complex and responsive to many factors. Distinctions in social understandings of specific industries and enterprises are relevant; the airline industry is not equivalent to the television business. The impact of gender conventions on employment opportunities is also pertinent. *Wilson* is a case about sex-specific hiring practices, whereas *Craft* concerns sex-specific ap-

113. *Id.*

114. *See* Alan Hyde, *Bodies of Law* 120 (1997).

115. The radical implications of the District of Columbia statute prohibiting discrimination on the basis of personal appearance have been contained by judicial interpretations that essentially follow the logic of *Craft. See* D.C. Code Ann. §§ 1-2501, 1-2502(22) (1999). The District of Columbia Court of Appeals accepts consumer preferences as constituting "a reasonable business purpose" for employer regulations of appearance. *See Turcios v. United States Serv. Indus.,* 680 A.2d 1023, 1029 (D.C. 1996) (finding that fear that contracts would be jeopardized was a sufficient reasonable business purpose for a no-tail hairstyle rule).

116. For a critique of *Craft, see* Note, "Sex Discrimination in Newscasting," 84 *Mich. L. Rev.* 443 (1985). *See* generally, Note, "Title VII Limits on Discrimination against Television Anchorwomen on the Basis of Age-Related Appearance," 85 *Colum. L. Rev.* 190 (1985).

pearance codes applied to a gender-integrated workforce.[117] The effect of accepting gender conventions is therefore different in the two cases. Also relevant, however, is a court's independent assessment of the value of the conventions potentially displaced by Title VII.

One can see this clearly in a case like *Fesel v. Masonic Home of Delaware, Inc.*,[118] which involved a residential retirement home that refused to hire male nurse's aides. The responsibilities of the aides included the provision of "intimate personal care, including dressing, bathing, toilet assistance, geriatric pad changes and catheter care."[119] Twenty-two of the home's thirty guests were female,[120] and many of these "would not consent to having their personal needs attended to by . . . male nurse's aides."[121] The court acknowledged the preferences of the home's customers and held that the "the sex of the nurse's aides at the Home is crucial to successful job performance."[122] The court did not deny that these preferences rested on "sexual stereotyping," but it nevertheless explicitly accepted these stereotypes as legitimate:

> As plaintiff stresses, the attitudes of the nonconsenting female guests at the Home are undoubtedly attributable to their upbringing and to sexual stereotyping of the past. While these attitudes may be characterized as "customer preference," this is, nevertheless, not the kind of case governed by the regulatory provision that customer preference alone cannot justify a job qualification based upon sex. Here personal privacy interests are implicated which are protected by law and which have to be recognized by the employer in running its business.[123]

---

117. For a recent decision involving sex-specific hiring practices for TV anchors, *see* Mike Allen, "Anchorwoman Wins $8.3 Million over Sex Bias," *N.Y. Times,* Jan. 29, 1999, at B1. Apparently, the TV station in that case insisted on pairing male and female anchors; it had refused to renew the plaintiff's contract because they had too many female anchors.

118. 447 F. Supp. 1346 (D. Del. 1978).

119. *Id.* at 1352–53.

120. *See id.* at 1348.

121. *Id.* at 1352.

122. *Id.* at 1353.

123. *Id.* at 1352. The court's point that the privacy interests of the guests are "protected by law" is simply makeweight, because the federal requirements of Title VII preempt any

Gender is highly salient in matters of privacy. The sex of the person by whom we are seen or touched normally matters very much to us. For this reason, the court in *Fesel* did not imagine the plaintiff as an individual whose sex was irrelevant, but instead as a fully sexed person. Even though the employer in *Fesel,* like the employer in *Wilson,* sought to maintain a single-sex work force, *Fesel* accepted the gender-specific stereotypes implicit in the privacy norms invoked by the nursing home, and the court incorporated these stereotypes into the BFOQ exception of Title VII.[124]

Fesel illustrates how Title VII does not simply displace gender practices, but rather interacts with them in a selective manner. The case forces us to ask which gender practices are to be reshaped by Title VII, in what contexts, and in what ways. These are questions that depend on our understanding of the exact purposes and ambitions of Title VII. They are also questions that depend on our assessment of the capacity of legal institutions to transform social practices. Any such assessment must depend on tact and judgment. As one court put it, "The laws outlawing sex discrimination are important. They are a significant advance. They must be realistically interpreted, or they will be ignored or displaced. Ours should not be an effort to achieve a unisex society." [125]

The many nuances of these inquiries are lost if Title VII is imagined simply as striking "at the entire spectrum of disparate treatment of men

---

competing considerations of state law. In *Rosenfeld v. Southern Pac. Co.,* for example, the court responded to the defendant's contention that "appointing a woman to the position would result in a violation of California labor laws and regulations which limit hours of work for women and restrict the weight they are permitted to lift," with the curt observation "that state labor laws inconsistent with the general objectives of the Act must be disregarded." 444 F.2d 1219, 1223, 1226 (9th Cir. 1971); *see also* 29 C.F.R. §1604.2(b) (1998).

124. On privacy as a BFOQ, *see Automobile Workers v. Johnson Controls, Inc.,* 499 U.S. 187, 206 n.4 (1991); *EEOC v. Sedita,* 816 F. Supp. 1291 (N.D. Ill. 1993); *Hernandez v. University of St. Thomas,* 793 F. Supp. 214 (D. Minn. 1992); *Local 567, AFSCME v. Michigan Council 25,* 635 F. Supp. 1010 (E.D. Mich. 1986); *EEOC v. Mercy Health Ctr.,* 29 FEP Cases 159 (W.D. Okl. 1982). For critiques, *see* Elsa M. Shartsis, "Privacy as Rationale for the Sex-Based BFOQ," 1985 *Det. C. L. Rev.* 865; Case Comment, "Sex Discrimination Justified under Title VII: Privacy Rights in Nursing Homes," 14 *Val. U. L. Rev.* 577 (1980).

125. *Boyce v. Safeway Stores,* 351 F. Supp. 402, 404 (D.D.C. 1972).

and women resulting from sex stereotypes."[126] This ambition is merely obfuscatory. It effaces, for example, the contrast between *Fesel* and a decision such as *Griffin v. Michigan Department of Corrections*,[127] in which women employees of all-male maximum security institutions in Michigan challenged a policy of prohibiting women from working within residential units. In *Griffin*, the court flatly rejected the state's claim that the policy was necessary to protect the privacy of male inmates. It castigated the policy as "based on a stereotypical sexual characterization that a viewing of an inmate while nude or performing bodily functions, by a member of the opposite sex, is intrinsically more odious than the viewing by a member of one's own sex."[128] *Griffin* explained that this was "just the type of stereotypical value system condemned by Title VII."[129] "The implicit mandate of Title VII is that a woman should be evaluated and treated by an employer on the basis of her individual qualifications and not on the basis of any assumptions regarding the characteristics and qualifications of women as a group."[130]

Griffin reproduces standard Title VII rhetoric and logic. But if we were to try to explain the different outcomes in *Fesel* and *Griffin*, this logic would seem unhelpful. Instead, we would certainly begin with the fact that *Fesel* addresses the privacy rights of nursing home residents, while *Griffin* assesses the privacy concerns of convicted criminals in maximum security institutions. Although gender stereotypes are equally present in both cases, so that the generic Title VII logic of

---

126. *County of Washington v. Gunther*, 452 U.S. 161, 180 (1981) (quoting *City of Los Angeles Dep't of Water & Power v. Manhart*, 435 U.S. 702, 707 n.13 [1978]) (quoting *Sprogis v. United Air Lines*, 444 F.2d 1194, 1198 [7th Cir. 1971]).

127. 654 F. Supp. 690 (E.D. Mich. 1982).

128. *Id.* at 701.

129. *Id.* at 702 (quoting *Gunther v. Iowa State Men's Reformatory*, 462 F. Supp. 952, 956 n.4 [N.D. Iowa 1979]).

130. *Id.* at 701. As a consequence of the holding and reasoning of *Griffin*, the state of Michigan subsequently authorized male guards to work in the residential units of female prisoners, and this policy resulted in charges of serious sexual harassment and abuse. *See* Human Rights Watch, "Nowhere To Hide: Retaliation against Women in Michigan State Prisons," 10 *Human Rights Watch Report* 2 (Sept. 1998); Human Rights Watch Women's Rights Project, *All Too Familiar: Sexual Abuse of Women in U.S. State Prisons* 242–80 (1996).

individualism is equally relevant, the courts evidently attributed less value to the gendered privacy norms of prisoners than to those of nursing home residents. This illustrates that as gender norms come to seem more fundamental to a court, it will be correspondingly more reluctant to disturb them. Norms that are fundamental are those that are significant and uncontroversial when seen from the perspective of those implementing the law.

A good example of norms that may seem superficially trivial but in fact are regarded as fundamental are those that involve the presentation of the self in matters of grooming and dress.[131] Gender is pervasively constituted by norms of presentation. It should therefore be no surprise that courts have generally held "that regulations promulgated by employers which require male employees to conform to different grooming and dress standards than female employees [are] not sex discrimination within the meaning of Title VII."[132] In the view of most courts, such regulations no more constitute discrimination "on the basis of sex . . . than a condition of employment that requires males and females to use separate toilet facilities."[133]

131. For a general discussion of these cases, *see* Katharine T. Bartlett, "Only Girls Wear Barrettes: Dress and Appearance Standards, Community Norms, and Workplace Equality," 92 *Mich. L. Rev.* 2541 (1994); Peter Brandon Bayer, "Mutable Characteristics and the Definition of Discrimination under Title VII," 20 *U.C. Davis L. Rev.* 769 (1987); Paulette M. Caldwell, "A Hair Piece: Perspectives on the Intersection of Race and Gender," 1991 *Duke L. J.* 365 (1991); Karl E. Klare, "Power/Dressing: Regulation of Employee Appearance," 26 *New Eng. L. Rev.* 1395 (1992); Lynne D. Mapes-Riordan, "Sex Discrimination and Employer Weight and Appearance Standards," 16 *Employee Rel. L. J.* 493 (1991); Mary Whisner, "Gender-Specific Clothing Regulation: A Study in Patriarchy," 5 *Harv. Women's L. J.* 73 (1982).

132. *Fountain v. Safeway Stores,* 555 F.2d 753, 755 (9th Cir. 1977). "The Act was never intended to interfere in the promulgation and enforcement of personal appearance regulations by private employers," because Congress could not have intended "for its proscription of sexual discrimination to have [such] significant and sweeping implications." *Knott v. Missouri Pac. R.R.,* 527 F.2d 1249, 1251–52 (8th Cir. 1975).

133. *Boyce v. Safeway Stores,* 351 F. Supp. 402, 403 (D.D.C. 1972); see also *Dodge v. Giant Food, Inc.,* 488 F.2d 1333, 1337 (D.C. Cir. 1973) (upholding distinct hair length requirements for men and women and mentioning sex-segregated toilet facilities as clearly outside the reach of Title VII). I should note that early in the history of Title VII there were a few decisions in which judges did attempt to use the law to displace gender norms of

*Grooming
And
Press* [handwritten margin note]

The striking authority exercised by gendered appearance norms in the interpretation of Title VII may be seen in a decision like *Lanigan v. Bartlett & Co. Grain.*[134] In that case the plaintiff attacked an employer's rule prohibiting women from wearing pants in its executive offices, alleging that the rule perpetuated "'a sexist, chauvinistic attitude'" that could not be functionally defended, because the company "'could offer no excuse whatsoever as to why [a] secretary could perform a job in a more efficient manner in a skirt rather than a pantsuit.'"[135] The court blandly replied to these stinging allegations that they "miss the point": "An employer is not required to justify any business practice in a Title VII action until and unless the plaintiff has established a prima facie case of discrimination. The fact that defendant introduced no evidence on the 'business necessity' of a dress code prohibiting pantsuits

---

dress and grooming. For example, in *Aros v. McDonnell Douglas Corp.*, 348 F. Supp. 661 (C.D. Cal. 1972), the court struck down a grooming code that permitted women, but not men, to have long hair. In an eloquent summary of the dominant view, the court said:

> The issue of long hair on men tends to arouse the passions of many in our society today. In that regard the issue is no different from issues of race, color, religion, national origin and equal employment rights for women, all of which are raised in Title VII. When this Nation was settled it was hoped that there be established a society where every individual would be judged according to his ability rather than who his father was, . . . or what the color of his skin was. Since then, millions of individuals have landed on our shores in search of opportunity — opportunity which was denied them in their homelands because of rigid class structures and irrational group stereotypes. The Civil Rights Act of 1964 was born of that hope. Although the legal technicalities are many, the message of the Act is clear: every person is to be treated as an individual, with respect and dignity. Stereotypes based upon race, color, religion, sex or national origin are to be avoided. . . . Males with long hair conjure up exactly the sort of stereotyped responses Congress intended to be discarded. . . . Some employers argue that their professional image and reputation may suffer from hiring men who prefer to wear their hair in longer styles. Title VII does not permit the employer to indulge in such generalizations. The Act requires that every individual be judged according to his own conduct and job performance.

Summary of view of long hair on men. [handwritten margin note]

Id. at 666; *see Donohue v. Shoe Corp. of Am.*, 337 F. Supp. 1357 (C.D. Cal. 1972) (denying defendant's motion to dismiss under Fed. R. Civ. P. 12(b)(6) in circumstances analogous to those in *Aros*).

134. 466 F. Supp. 1388 (W.D. Mo. 1979).

135. *Id.* at 1391.

Grooming and dress

on women working in its executive offices proves nothing because the Court holds that plaintiff has not established a prima facie case of discrimination. Accordingly, defendant was not obligated to defend its dress code policies."[136]

Title VII decisions distinguish between grooming and dress codes that track "generally accepted community standards of dress and appearance"[137] and those that do not. The former are regarded as enforcing a "neutral" baseline that negates any inference of sex discrimination.[138] Thus an employer who requires employees "to be neatly dressed and groomed in accordance with the standards customarily accepted in the business community," and hence who excludes "the employing of men (but not women) with long hair," does not discriminate on the basis of sex in violation of Title VII.[139]

Employer dress codes that violate traditional standards, however, are regarded as enforcing sex discrimination. Thus the dress code of an employer who permitted men to wear "customary business attire" but who required women to wear a "uniform" was regarded as without "justification in commonly accepted social norms."[140] It was consequently rejected as "demeaning," as embodying the "offensive stereotypes prohibited by Title VII."[141] This conclusion obtains whether or not female employees can demonstrate any other material differences in their treatment (i.e., in their "salary, benefits, hours of employment, raises, employment evaluations or any other term or condition of employment").[142]

These cases nicely illustrate how customary gender norms are incorporated into the very meaning and texture of Title VII.[143] So far

136. *Id.*

137. *Willingham v. Macon Tel. Pub. Co.*, 507 F.2d 1084, 1092 (5th Cir. 1975).

138. *See id.* at 1092.

139. *Id.* at 1087.

140. *Carroll v. Talman Fed. Sav. & Loan Ass'n*, 604 F.2d 1028, 1029, 1032 (7th Cir. 1979).

141. *Id.* at 1033.

142. *O'Donnell v. Burlington Coat Factory Warehouse, Inc.*, 656 F. Supp. 263, 265 (S.D. Ohio 1987).

143. The point, of course, may be made about the law more generally. Thus in defending a judge's policy of requiring male attorneys, but not female attorneys, to wear ties in court, a federal judge concluded: "At least until that dreadful day when unisex iden-

*Grooming
And
dress*

from striking "at the entire spectrum of disparate treatment of men and women resulting from sex stereotypes,"[144] the statute in fact negotiates the ways in which it will shape and alter existing gender norms. So long as gender conventions remain salient within our culture, Title VII must be understood as marking a frontier between those gender conventions subject to legal transformation and those left untouched or actually reproduced within the law. The frontier is of course a moving one, for courts are continuously reevaluating which stereotypes should be permitted, in what contexts, and for what reasons. We can be certain, however, that to the extent that gender remains a culturally inescapable fact, it also will remain inextricably present in the application of Title VII.[145]

It may be useful to recapitulate the argument that I have so far developed. The dominant conception of American antidiscrimination law aspires to suppress categories of social judgment that are deemed likely to be infected with prejudice. This suppression occurs within an imaginative space that figures a correspondence between presocial individuals, on the one hand, and "context-free" functional capacities on the other. There is thus a strong impulse within the dominant perspective to imagine the law as standing in a neutral space outside of history and of the contingent social practices of which history is comprised.

Taken to its ultimate conclusion, the utopian quality of this impulse

---

tity of dress and appearance arrives, judicial officers . . . are entitled to some latitude in differentiating between male and female attorneys, within the context of decorous professional behavior and appearance. . . . Because contemporary fashions are different, a judge may permissibly conclude that a male attorney appearing in court without a necktie is lacking in proper decorum, whereas a female attorney not wearing a necktie is not subject to that criticism." *Devine v. Lonschein,* 621 F. Supp. 894, 897 (S.D.N.Y. 1985).

144. *County of Washington v. Gunther,* 452 U.S. 161, 180 (1981) (quoting *City of Los Angeles Dep't of Water & Power v. Manhart,* 435 U.S. 702, 707 n.13 [1978]) (quoting *Sprogis v. United Air Lines, Inc.,* 444 F.2d 1194, 1198 [7th Cir. 1971]).

145. For an incisive formulation of this point in the context of legal interventions into matters of gender generally, *see* Reva B. Siegel, "Home as Work: The First Woman's Rights Claims Concerning Wives' Household Labor, 1850–1880," 103 *Yale L. J.* 1073, 1212–15 (1994).

suggests why TRB was so unsettled by the prospect of prohibiting discrimination on the basis of personal appearance. Anti-lookism ordinances abstract so severely from everyday social life that it is difficult to imagine how they could possibly reconstruct any actual social practice. We might even go so far as to say that the Santa Cruz ordinance would be inconceivable unless one were, so to speak, in the grip of the dominant conception.

Because the dominant conception offers an implausible story about the actual shape of antidiscrimination law, I have proposed an alternative perspective, which we may call the sociological account, in which antidiscrimination law is understood as a social practice that acts on other social practices. According to the sociological account, antidiscrimination law must be seen as transforming preexisting social practices, such as race or gender, by reconstructing the social identities of persons.[146] The sociological account does not ask whether "stereotypic impressions" can be eliminated tout court, but rather how the law alters and modifies such impressions.

In contrast to the dominant conception, the sociological account accepts the inevitability of social practices. But precisely because of this acceptance, the account requires that principles be articulated that will guide and direct the transformation of social practices. Because the dominant conception seeks entirely to transcend and eliminate social practices, it has not fully developed such principles. Instead, it imagines a world in which the presocial demands of an "original position" exactly coincide with the imperatives of a "context-free" functional rationality. It therefore lacks the resources to identify and analyze the many ways in which instrumental rationality can itself actually reinforce existing social practices. The sociological account, by contrast, focuses on how the law reconstructs social practices, even at the sacrifice of instrumental rationality.

146. An antidiscrimination law informed by the sociological account would thus not approach the problem of lookism by attempting to make us blind to appearances, but rather "by directing attention to" and seeking to alter "oppressive social norms of beauty." Elizabeth S. Anderson, "What Is the Point of Equality?," 109 *Ethics* 287, 335 (1999).

Of course, the practical impact of the sociological account will depend on the nature of the specific principles that we seek to implement through antidiscrimination law.[147] The insights that the sociological account offers concerning the actual operation of antidiscrimination law, however, ought to be pertinent to the adoption of these principles. In this regard, it is useful to bear in mind that although the articulation of such principles will transpire chiefly through the usual mechanisms of statutory and constitutional interpretation, larger moral values will no doubt also prove influential. The sociological account therefore need not prove intrinsically incompatible with normative reasoning or even with the heuristic device of the original position. But we can learn from the sociological account that insofar as we seek to realize the conclusions of normative reasoning in law, we should do so in a way that recognizes how law functions to embody itself in history.

In this brief essay, I shall not attempt to argue for any particular set of principles that ought to guide the application of antidiscrimination law. That is too long and complicated a discussion. I shall instead explore the question of whether it makes any difference if we substitute the understanding of the actual operation of antidiscrimination law contained in the sociological account for that implicit within the dominant conception, even on the assumption that we have not yet specified any such principles. The dominant conception, after all, tells a simple and powerful story that has successfully propelled important changes in American society. Even if it is in some ways incomplete and inaccurate, we nevertheless ought to be careful about abandoning such

147. Much of the scholarly work on antisubordination theory can be interpreted as advocating principles that could guide the application of antidiscrimination law under a sociological approach. *See, e.g.,* Ruth Colker, "Anti-Subordination Above All: Sex, Race, and Equal Protection," 61 *N.Y.U. L. Rev.* 1003, 1005 (1986); Kimberle Williams Crenshaw, "Race, Reform, and Retrenchment: Transformation and Legitimation in Antidiscrimination Law," 101 *Harv. L. Rev.* 1331 (1988). But antisubordination theory is by no means the only source for such principles. There is a wide range of possibilities. Each of Barbara Flagg's opposed notions of the "pluralist" and "assimilationist" interpretation of equal opportunity could, for example, potentially serve this purpose. *See* Flagg, *supra* note 51, at 2033–36.

an effective instrument of social transformation. Four considerations seem to me especially pertinent to assessing the advisability of any such course of action.

First, I think it clear that the insights of the sociological account can create greater judicial accountability than can the dominant conception. The sociological account suggests that courts will apply antidiscrimination law in ways that implicate it in the very practices it seeks to modify. The dominant conception, however, denies that these practices have any legitimate role in the application of antidiscrimination law. If, in fact, the sociological account is correct, we can expect judicial opinions to reach conclusions that accept social practices in implicit and indirect ways. This is certainly evident in a decision such as *Craft*,[148] where the dominant conception stripped the court of its ability to acknowledge the legitimacy of gender norms, and where the court was therefore forced to smuggle its acceptance of these norms into an instrumental logic that deferred to consumer preferences. By contrast, an approach that accepted the insights of the sociological account would have invited the court in *Craft* explicitly to state and defend the grounds for its conclusions, and this in turn would have facilitated public review and critique. Such an approach would thus render decisions such as *Craft* far more accountable for their actual judgments.

In a similar way, the insights of the sociological account would render more accountable decisions like *Wilson*[149] or the EEOC judgment in the courier guard case.[150] Each of these decisions involves contexts in which functional rationality potentially undermines a norm of gender blindness. Yet because the dominant conception lacks the resources to analyze or acknowledge such a tension, both opinions were led systematically to manipulate the category of functional rationality so as to disguise its divergence from the norm of gender blindness. As a result, neither opinion could offer a frank and helpful discussion of how such contradictions ought to be resolved. Because the sociological account finds no particular discomfort in recognizing that the project of

---

148. 766 F.2d 1205 (8th Cir. 1985); see *supra* notes 110–117 and accompanying text.
149. See *supra* notes 103–108 and accompanying text.
150. See *supra* notes 97–101 and accompanying text.

transforming gender conventions may sometimes require the sacrifice of instrumental rationality, it would invite a more candid appraisal of the trade-offs implicit in such situations. Accountability would thereby be increased.

Second, the insights of the sociological account would for this reason encourage greater doctrinal coherence. It is potentially damaging to the structure of the law when judges cannot explain the actual justifications for their decisions.[151] The point is well illustrated by the Title VII cases involving gender-specific grooming codes. Such codes clearly regulate persons who have socially endowed gender identities, rather than "individuals" for whom sex is irrelevant. They are for this reason anomalous within the framework of the dominant conception. Yet American judges, who tend to be quite practical,[152] have been unwilling to use Title VII to strike down these codes. Caught between a doctrinal commitment to the dominant conception and an instinctive apprehension that Title VII should be understood as modifying (rather than displacing) gender norms, courts have been unable to offer any coherent doctrinal explanation of their decisions.

Perhaps the leading case is *Willingham v. Macon Telegraph Publishing Co.*,[153] in which a newspaper required male but not female employees to have short hair. Willingham held that the newspaper's grooming code was an example of " 'sex plus' discrimination" because it was on the basis "of sex plus one other ostensibly neutral characteristic" (short hair) that the newspaper discriminated against some men, but not all men.[154] The court concluded that " 'sex plus' discrimination" was not discrimination on the basis of sex for purpose of Title VII unless the "plus" factor involved "immutable characteristics" or a "fundamental right" (such as the right to marry).[155]

---

151. I acknowledge, however, that there are sometimes important legal values to be served by judicial indirection, by the ability of courts to pursue their ends in implicit and inarticulate ways. *See, e.g.,* Robert C. Post, "Reconceptualizing Vagueness: Legal Rules and Social Orders," 82 *Calif. L. Rev.* 491, 507 (1994).

152. *See, e.g., supra* note 125 and accompanying text.

153. 507 F.2d 1084 (5th Cir. 1975).

154. *Id.* at 1089.

155. *Id.* at 1091. The court thus distinguished *Sprogis v. United Airlines,* 444 F.2d 1194 (7th

This doctrine of "sex plus" discrimination is broadly framed and carries a wide range of potential applications. It has been consequential,[156] and yet it is entirely incoherent. If an employer imposes a grooming code that requires blacks, but not whites, to have short hair, I strongly suspect that no court in the country would classify the code as "race plus" and hence immune from Title VII scrutiny. *Willingham* justifies the requirement that the plus factor be either an immutable characteristic or a fundamental right on the grounds that only such factors are important enough to interfere with the "equal employment opportunity" that is said to be the essential purpose of Title VII.[157] But this justification is plainly misconceived. If an employer requires female but not male employees to live within three miles of a factory, the requirement would affect equal employment opportunity but involve neither an immutable characteristic nor a fundamental right.[158]

What seems in fact to be driving the outcome in Willingham is the conviction that employers reasonably may impose sex-based stereotypes in matters of grooming, so long as these stereotypes conform to traditional gender conventions. That explains why courts confronting dress codes that find "no justification in accepted social norms" have struck them down, even though the codes cause no discernible adverse effects on other equal employment opportunities.[159] But courts never

---

Cir. 1971), in which a requirement that female airline stewardesses be unmarried was found to violate Title VII.

156. *See, e.g., Jefferies v. Harris County Community Action Ass'n,* 615 F.2d 1025, 1033 (5th Cir. 1980); *Earwood v. Continental Southeastern Lines,* 539 F.2d 1349, 1351 (4th Cir. 1976); *Arnett v. Aspin,* 846 F. Supp. 1234, 1239 (E.D. Pa. 1994); *Lanigan v. Bartlett & Co. Grain,* 466 F. Supp. 1388, 1391 (W.D. Mo. 1979); *cf. Coleman v. B-G Maintenance Management of Colo., Inc.,* 108 F.3d 1199, 1203–04 (10th Cir. 1997); *Rogers v. American Airlines,* 527 F. Supp. 229, 231 (S.D.N.Y. 1981); *Jarrell v. Eastern Air Lines,* 430 F. Supp. 884, 892 (E.D. Va. 1977).

157. 507 F.2d at 1091.

158. The example is drawn from the dissenting opinion of Judge Winter in *Earwood. See* 539 F.2d at 1352 n.2.

159. *O'Donnell v. Burlington Coat Factory Warehouse, Inc.,* 656 F. Supp. 263, 265–66 (S.D. Ohio 1987); *see also Carroll v. Talman Fed. Sav. & Loan Ass'n of Chicago,* 604 F.2d 1028 (7th Cir. 1979).

[handwritten: ✳ Grooming]

directly address the fundamental question of why the gender roles implicit in dress codes reasonably may be imposed when they reflect conventional standards.

It seems to be important that grooming and dress codes regulate voluntary behavior, for courts tend to conceptualize employees who present themselves in ways that violate established gender grooming and dress conventions as asserting a "personal preference" to flout accepted standards.[160] Courts therefore read claims for protection by those who deviate from gendered appearance norms as ultimately asserting a right autonomously to present oneself "in a self-determined manner,"[161] rather than a right to fair and equal treatment.[162] Just as Santa Cruz employers bridled at having to accept people who "look and act as if they don't care what others think,"[163] so federal courts have been unwilling to require employers to ignore what they regard as willful deviations from customary norms of gender appearance.[164]

The dominant conception, however, prevents courts from explicitly articulating doctrinal rules that express this perspective. This is because the dominant conception holds that all employer decisions "motivated

160. *Earwood,* 539 F.2d at 1351.

161. *Fagan v. National Cash Register Co.,* 481 F.2d 1115, 1117 (D.C. Cir. 1973).

162. This tendency may account for the otherwise mysterious tendency of courts to say that gendered norms of appearance do not violate Title VII because the statute only prohibits discrimination based on "immutable characteristics." *Baker v. California Land Title Co.,* 507 F.2d 895, 897 (9th Cir. 1974); *cf. Bedker v. Domino's Pizza, Inc.,* 62 FEP Cases 1848 (1992). Title VII, of course, prohibits discrimination based on religion, which is not immutable. For a discussion, see *supra* text at notes 36–40.

163. *Adams, supra* note 22, at C4 (quoting businessman Nole Smith).

164. As the court said in *Fagan,* 481 F.2d at 1124–25,

Perhaps no facet of business life is more important than a company's place in public estimation. That the image created by its employees dealing with the public when on company assignment affects its relations is so well known that we may take judicial notice of an employer's proper desire to achieve favorable acceptance. Good grooming regulations reflect a company's policy in our highly competitive business environment. Reasonable requirements in furtherance of that policy are an aspect of managerial responsibility.

[handwritten: Company's place in public estimation]

For a defense of employee autonomy in the context of dress and grooming codes, see Klare, *supra* note 131.

Grooming
& Gender Norms

by stereotypical notions" about proper gender "deportment" are presumptively illegal.[165] We are therefore simultaneously confronted by the spectacle of preposterous doctrinal formulations and deprived of the vigorous debate that would surely surround the reasons for the grooming and dress code cases were they to be explicitly defended. Not only is

165. *Price Waterhouse v. Hopkins,* 490 U.S. 228, 256 (1989) (Brennan, J., plurality opinion). In *Price Waterhouse,* a woman was denied partnership at a large accounting firm because, it was said, she "should 'walk more femininely, talk more femininely, dress more femininely, wear make-up, have her hair styled, and wear jewelry.' " *Id.* at 235. The Court condemned the denial as based on "sex stereotyping," which it held was illegal because " 'in forbidding employers to discriminate against individuals because of their sex, Congress intended to strike at the entire spectrum of disparate treatment of men and women resulting from sex stereotypes.' " *Id.* at 251 (quoting *City of Los Angeles Dep't of Water & Power v. Manhart,* 435 U.S. 702, 707 n.13 [1978]) (quoting *Sprogis v. United Air Lines,* 444 F.2d 1194, 1198 [7th Cir. 1971]). *Price Waterhouse* perfectly exemplifies the dominant conception. It sets forth a simple and powerful principle that would obliterate gender conventions.

How far we are from any such likelihood may be seen in cases such as *Smith v. Liberty Mutual Ins. Co.,* 569 F.2d 325 (5th Cir. 1978), which refused to extend Title VII protection to claims of discrimination on the basis of effeminacy. *Smith* in fact uses *Willingham's* "sex plus" doctrine, see *supra* notes 153–155 and accompanying text, to reject the claim of a man who argued that he had been "discriminated against because . . . as a male, he was thought to have those attributes more generally characteristic of females and epitomized in the descriptive 'effeminate.' " *Id.* at 327. Despite *Hopkins, Smith* is still regarded by "courts and commentators . . . as good law." Mary Anne C. Case, "Disaggregating Gender from Sex and Sexual Orientation: The Effeminate Man in the Law and Feminist Jurisprudence," 105 *Yale L. J.* 1, 3 n.3 (1995); *see also* Barbara Lindemann, Paul Grossman, and Paul W. Cane Jr., *I Employment Discrimination Law* 475–78 (3d ed. 1996). It remains more or less standard Title VII doctrine that the statute does not prohibit employer actions enforcing stereotypic masculine roles, as, for example, by barring men from wearing earrings, on the grounds that "discrimination because of effeminacy, like discrimination because of homosexuality . . . or transsexualism . . . does not fall within the purview of Title VII." *DeSantis v. Pacific Tel. and Tel. Co.,* 608 F.2d 327, 332 (9th Cir. 1979); *see also Williamson v. A. G. Edwards & Sons,* 876 F.2d 69 (8th Cir. 1989); *Dobre v. National R.R. Passenger Corp.,* 850 F. Supp. 284, 286–87 (E.D. Pa. 1993). For an able discussion, *see* Case, *supra,* at 36–75. For examples of similar holdings in antidiscrimination contexts other than Title VII, *see Rathert v. Village of Peotone,* 903 F.2d 510, 516 (7th Cir. 1990), cert. denied, 498 U.S. 921 (1990) (upholding prohibition on earrings for male police officers); *Star v. Gramley,* 815 F. Supp. 276, 278–79 (C.D. Ill. 1993) (upholding prohibition on women's garb and make-up for male prison inmate).

the law stripped of accountability, but the internal architecture and integrity of the law, which is sustained by clear and purposeful doctrine, is undermined.

Coherent doctrine is important because it is the means by which law directs courts to issues that are pertinent for legal intervention. My third observation, therefore, is that the understandings brought to bear by the sociological account will tend to focus judicial attention on what seems to me the right question, the question that ought to govern the application of antidiscrimination law. If the point of antidiscrimination law is to transform existing social practices, then courts must ask what purpose the law expects to accomplish by such transformations. The dominant conception systematically obscures this question.[166] If the aim of the law is not in fact to strike "at the entire spectrum of disparate treatment of men and women resulting from sex stereotypes,"[167] then what is it?

Antidiscrimination law would be greatly advanced if it were simply to pose this question in a sharp and useful way. We could then see, for

166. Consider, for example, the EEOC's 1969 explication of the BFOQ standard, which states that "jobs may be restricted to members of one sex"

For reasons of authenticity (actress, actor, model)

Because of community standards of morality or propriety (restroom attendant, lingerie sales clerk)

In jobs in the entertainment industry for which sex appeal is an essential qualification.

EEOC, *Toward Job Equality for Women* 5 (1969). The EEOC emphasized, however, that "jobs may not be restricted to members of one sex" because of "Assumptions related to the applicant's sex . . . [or] Preferences of co-workers, employers, clients or customers." *Id.* We are thus instructed by the EEOC that gender discrimination is acceptable because of "propriety," but unacceptable because of "preferences." An employer may engage in gender discrimination to uphold "community standards of morality," but not to sustain "assumptions related to the applicant's sex." These distinctions are obviously obscure; they can be illuminated only through a clear explication of the aims and aspirations of Title VII. But because the dominant conception denies these distinctions, it also suppresses any such effort at explication. As a consequence, the law is left as confused and as incomplete as this EEOC pronouncement.

167. *County of Washington v. Gunther*, 452 U.S. 161, 180 (1981) (quoting *Los Angeles Dep't of Water & Power v. Manhart*, 435 U.S. 702, 707 n. 13 [1978]) (quoting *Sprogis v. United Air Lines*, 444 F.2d 1194, 1198 [7th Cir. 1971]).

example, that the ambitions of the law vary depending on the social practice at issue. To pick an obvious example, if the nursing home residents in *Fesel* had claimed a privacy right not to be touched by nurse's aides who were African American, their expectations would no doubt properly and ruthlessly be overridden by Title VII. This is because antidiscrimination law seeks to exercise a far more sweeping transformation of race than of gender, as is evident in the fact that Title VII does not even contain a BFOQ exception for race.[168] We are evidently more

168. Because race, like sex, actually matters in social life, the absence of a BFOQ for race sometimes leads to anomalous results. During the legislative debates over Title VII, for example, Senator Dirksen raised the question of "a movie company making an extravaganza on Africa [which] may well decide to have hundreds of extras of a particular race or color to make the movie as authentic as possible." 110 *Cong. Rec.* 7217 (1964). Senator Clark, a floor manager for the statute, replied in a memorandum that "a director of a play or movie who wished to cast an actor in the role of a Negro, could specify that he wished to hire someone with the physical appearance of a Negro—but such a person might actually be a non-Negro. Therefore, the act would not limit the director's freedom of choice." *Id.* Clark's response is notable on a number of grounds. First, it is flatly evasive. An employer could not escape Title VII's prohibitions simply by advertising for employees who "appear" to be white. Second, Clark's memorandum seems to define race as a biological fact, rather than as a socially constructed phenotype or "appearance." (I am grateful to Reva Siegel for this observation.) It is thus entirely unresponsive to Dirksen's inquiry if one believes that race is not a biological fact but a social construction and hence ultimately rooted in social appearance. *See* Robert Post, "Racist Speech, Democracy, and the First Amendment," 32 *Wm. & Mary L. Rev.* 267, 296–97 (1991). Third, because Title VII also prohibits discrimination on the basis of color, Senator Clark seems also to imply some differentiation between "color" and the "appearance" of race. For a discussion of Title VII and discrimination on the basis of "color," *see* Sara Scott, "A New Category of 'Color': Analyzing Albinism under Title VII and the Americans With Disabilities Act," 2 *J. Gender, Race & Just.* 493 (1999). In sum, the continuing salience of race in society, coupled with Title VII's uncompromising suppression of race as a ground of decision making, renders the plight of the movie company genuinely puzzling. Yet contemporary courts continue to reaffirm the *Clark* rationale in such cases. *See, e.g., Ferrill v. Parker Group, Inc.,* 168 F.3d 468, 474 n.10 (11th Cir. 1999). There is evidence in the legislative history of Title VII that the statute was not directed against appearance, at least in the context of lookism. See, for example, the following dialogue between Senators Talmadge and Tower:

MR. TALMADGE. Would it be considered to be discrimination if a person wished to employ a good-looking stenographer instead of an unattractive stenographer?

determined to imagine individuals without race than we are individuals without sex.[169] Although clearly grasping such differences is a prerequisite for antidiscrimination law to achieve its ends, these differences are difficult even to formulate within the dominant conception.

This brings me to my fourth and concluding observation. Within the dominant conception, explicit racial or gender classifications stand as markers of the very potential for prejudice that creates the need for antidiscrimination law. These classifications are thus rendered deeply suspect because they are incompatible with the creation of individuals for whom race and gender are irrelevant. Immanent within the dominant conception, therefore, lies an almost irrepressible impulse to eliminate such classifications.

The impulse is so powerful that even in cases in which courts recognize the inevitability of such classifications, as in the gendered grooming cases, courts nevertheless cannot bring themselves to acknowledge that they are accepting explicit gender categories. The impulse is particularly puissant in cases dealing with affirmative action, and this creates odd theoretical tensions. For example, many of the very persons who would clearly perceive the limitations of the dominant conception when manifested in the Santa Cruz ordinance, and who would dismiss that ordinance as absurd, would also resist affirmative action on the basis of a visceral opposition to explicit racial and gender categories that flows directly from the dominant conception.

A virtue of the sociological account is that it has the capacity to tame this irresistible impulse to suppress explicit racial and gender classifications. If antidiscrimination law were to reorient itself around the

---

MR. TOWER. I have always tried to exercise that kind of discrimination in my hiring practice, and I suppose it is discriminatory. Of course, the bill provides that there shall be no discrimination on the basis of race, color, religion, national origin, or sex. It does not say anything about good looks. However, I am sure that none of the other terms are defined in the bill, either. 110 CONG. REC. 9026 (1964)

169. See Anthony Appiah, " 'But Would That Still Be Me?' " Notes on Gender, 'Race,' Ethnicity, as Sources of 'Identity,' " 87 J. Phil. 493, 497 (1990). (" 'Racial' ethical identities are for us . . . apparently less conceptually central to who one is than gender ethical identities.")

project of purposively reshaping the social practices of race and gender, explicit racial or gender classifications may or may not be suspect, depending on whether they affect race or gender practices in ways that are compatible with the objectives of the law.

This is exactly the perspective adopted by the Supreme Court when it was forced to face the difficult and controversial question of whether Title VII prohibited the use of explicit racial and gender classifications for purposes of affirmative action. In *United Steelworkers v. Weber*[170] and *Johnson v. Transportation Agency*,[171] Justice Brennan, writing for the Court, reasoned from "the historical context"[172] of the Act to analyze the relationship between such classifications and what he took to be the Act's purpose, which was "to break down old patterns of . . . segregation and hierarchy."[173] Whether or not one agrees with Brennan's controversial use of legislative history, and whether or not one agrees with his characterization of the ultimate goal of Title VII,[174] Brennan's great achievement in these cases was to break through the usual Title VII rhetoric of "stereotypes"[175] to engage in precisely the kind of inquiry that the sociological account would encourage. By shaking free of the dominant conception, Brennan was able directly to query the nature of the law's aims in seeking historically to transform existing practices of race and gender. Unfortunately, however, Brennan's opinions in *Weber* and *Johnson* remain isolated instances within a jurisprudence that still speaks as though race and gender could be placed behind a screen and made to disappear.

The impulse to suppress explicit racial and gender classifications is highly pronounced in decisions interpreting the Equal Protection

---

170. 443 U.S. 193 (1979).

171. 480 U.S. 616 (1987).

172. *Weber,* 443 U.S. at 201.

173. *Id.* at 208; *Johnson,* 480 U.S. at 628 (quoting *Weber,* 443 U.S. at 208).

174. On the controversial nature of Brennan's interpretation of Title VII, compare Ronald Dworkin, "How to Read the Civil Rights Act," in *A Matter of Principle* 316 (1985), with Bernard D. Meltzer, "The Weber Case: The Judicial Abrogation of the Antidiscrimination Standard in Employment," 47 *U. Chi. L. Rev.* 423 (1980).

175. *See City of Los Angeles Dep't of Water & Power v. Manhart,* 435 U.S. 702, 707–09 (1978).

Clause of the U.S. Constitution. It is fair to read the constitutional manifestation of this impulse as also reflecting (at least in part) the influence
of the dominant conception.[176] Constitutional opinions regularly express the ambition to erase "stereotypic notions"[177] by requiring the
state to focus on "individual men and women"[178] for whom race and
gender would be "irrelevant."[179] The urge to transcend history is thus
frequently apparent in the rhetoric of these opinions.

One possible consequence of the dominant conception within constitutional jurisprudence is the line of cases that scrutinize laws that
employ racial or gender classifications on their face differently than laws
that are facially neutral. It is standard constitutional doctrine that the
former should receive stringent and frequently fatal judicial review,[180]
whereas the latter should receive at best cursory consideration.[181] This
is true even for those facially neutral laws that have significantly retro-
grade effects on practices of race or gender.[182] This is odd doctrine,
however, if the purpose of antidiscrimination law is to transform these
practices.

I strongly suspect that the insights of the sociological account would
soften this sharp and consequential distinction between facially neutral
laws and laws that employ explicit racial and gender classifications. The
sociological account both deemphasizes the singularity of racial and
gender classifications and enhances the visibility of the multiple ways

176. See *supra* note 43 and accompanying text.

177. *Mississippi Univ. for Women v. Hogan*, 458 U.S. 718, 725 (1982).

178. *City of Richmond v. J. A. Croson Co.*, 488 U.S. 469, 528 (1989) (Scalia, J., concurring).

179. *Id.* at 527 (Scalia, J., concurring) (quoting Alexander Bickel, *The Morality of Consent*
133 [1975]).

180. *See United States v. Virginia*, 518 U.S. 515 (1996); *Adarand Constructors, Inc. v. Pena*,
515 U.S. 200 (1995).

181. *See Village of Arlington Heights v. Metropolitan Housing Dev. Corp.*, 429 U.S. 252
(1977). Such laws are scrutinized to determine if they have a discriminatory purpose.
See Hunter v. Underwood, 471 U.S. 222 (1985). Because of "disparate impact" analysis,
Title VII law is a good deal more sensitive than constitutional law about the effect of
facially neutral regulations on practices of gender and race. See *supra* note 51.

182. *See Personnel Admin. v. Feeney*, 442 U.S. 256, 270 (1979) (upholding constitutionality of state statute favoring veterans in civil service hiring despite fact that over 98
percent of benefited class was male).

in which facially neutral laws affect existing practices of race and gender. It thus encourages us to inquire whether these effects are consistent
or inconsistent with the purposes of the Equal Protection Clause. Of
course, on reflection, we might come to believe that the purposes of
the Equal Protection Clause are not to modify existing practices of race
and gender, but instead to reshape governmental processes of decision
making in ways oblivious to their effects on these practices.[183] But this
is precisely the kind of debate that we ought explicitly to engage.

We have traveled a long distance from our initial consideration of Santa
Cruz's strange anti-lookism ordinance. The eccentricity of that law enabled us to register unease at the project of systematically effacing the
social world. Yet we can now see that this same project also underlies
the general self-conception of American antidiscrimination law. As an
alternative to that project, therefore, I have offered an account of antidiscrimination law as an institutional intervention designed to transform, rather than to transcend, existing practices of gender and race. I
have discussed four considerations bearing on the practical differences
between these two ways of imagining the design of antidiscrimination
law. These considerations sound roughly in the dimensions of accountability, doctrinal integrity, purposive clarity, and an obsessive and dys-
functional focus on explicit racial classifications.

I do not insist that these considerations compel us to abandon the
dominant conception, for the latter has served us well over the years in
driving important and far-reaching changes in the social practices of
gender and race. The point is certainly debatable. But I do insist that
the sociological account more accurately captures how antidiscrimination law actually functions. Judges have in fact been compelled systematically to disguise and contort their judgments so as to render them
compatible with the surface logic of the dominant conception.

183. Alternatively, we might also conclude that, having assimilated the insights of the
sociological account, facially neutral laws would reshape existing practices of race and
gender in ways more consistent with constitutional imperatives than laws that employ
explicit racial and gender classifications. *See* Robert Post, "Introduction: After Bakke,"
in *Race and Representation: Affirmative Action* 18–20 (Robert Post and Michael Rogin
eds., 1998).

An alternative approach is suggested by the Court's controversial opinions in *Weber* and *Johnson,* which escape this compulsion by forthrightly accepting a framework of analysis that incorporates the basic understanding of antidiscrimination law advanced by the sociological account. It is my hope that this essay has enabled us to recognize the significance of that achievement and to pose in an intelligible way the question of whether it is an accomplishment we should desire to emulate.

K. Anthony Appiah | Stereotypes and the Shaping of Identity

I have spent a good deal of time over the years thinking about how our racial identities should figure in our moral and political lives—reflecting, that is, on the ethical significance of one dimension of difference.[1] I have thought about these questions as a moral philosopher and not as a legal theorist, and so I have not had to work within the constraints imposed by the law and the history of its interpretation. The advantage of this freedom is that one may reflect on how things should be, unconstrained by the necessity of deference to the confusions of the executive, legislative, and judicial branches of our government. The disadvantage is that one can find oneself proposing norms or practices that have no chance at all of being implemented and giving advice that seems, in the justly derogatory sense, "merely theoretical." So it is cheering to find someone like Professor Post, who both recognizes an important moral truth about the ethical significance of difference and believes that it

1. *See, e.g.,* K. Anthony Appiah, *In My Father's House: Africa in the Philosophy of Culture* (1992); K. Anthony Appiah and Amy Gutmann, *Color Conscious: The Political Morality of Race* (1996).

can be brought to bear in the practical business of interpreting actually existing American antidiscrimination law.

The moral truth I have in mind is the importance of a distinction that is at the heart of Post's characteristically elegant essay, that between treating people equally on the one hand, and treating them as if they were the same on the other—the distinction, as one might put it, between equality and sameness. The Vonnegut story he quotes rightly represents as wildly dystopian a world in which everyone is pushed toward sameness.[2] This story should make us suspicious of that interpretation of equality as an ideal.

Professor Post does a thoroughly convincing job of showing how unhelpful the picture of equality as sameness has been. He urges on us an approach in which, rather than pretending that difference does not exist, we take on, in part through legal action, the social reshaping of identities. The cases he explores center on gender, though he makes important observations along the way about race; but the conclusion he wants to draw applies to both of them and to other forms of identity, such as sexual orientation and disability as well. He wants us to think of the project of antidiscrimination in all of these cases as one of reshaping identities rather than ignoring them. But he does not say very much— and he says nothing directly and explicitly—about what norms should guide this reshaping.[3] So I shall try, in the next part, to sketch in some features of a more direct and explicit account. I do not propose a general account of the ways in which it is appropriate to seek to reshape identities.[4] But I want to say enough to connect the question of antidiscrimination with some central liberal ideas—in particular, in part II, with autonomy, dignity, and individuality. Against this background, in part III, I will then take up the issue of "stereotypes." Here I shall be more explicitly critical than Post is of current judicial *façons de parler:* For I think the way this word is used conflates a number of distinct

2. *See* Robert Post, "Prejudicial Appearances: The Logic of American Antidiscrimination Law," reproduced in this volume, pp. 1–53.

3. In fact, he says that he will "not attempt to argue for any particular set of principles that ought to guide the application of antidiscrimination law." *See* p. 41.

4. Amy Gutmann and I have discussed some of the issues at stake elsewhere. See Appiah and Gutmann, *supra* note 1.

issues.[5] In part IV, I make some concluding observations about why affirmative action, in the form of racial or gender preferences, need not be inconsistent with antidiscrimination properly construed—that is, as Post and (as he points out) Justice Brennan in *Weber*[6] both construe it.

The best way, I think, to grasp the power of the idea of equality is to think about the past practices against which those who have espoused the ideal were reacting. Slavery, Jim Crow, and what John Stuart Mill called the "Subjection of Women"[7]; the denial of civic rights to ethnic and religious minorities and to homosexuals; systems of caste and class: All these have evoked an ideal of equality in counterreaction to them. This suggests to me that it is not disparate treatment as such—not merely treating a member of class A differently from a member of class B—but rather some fairly specific kinds of disparate treatment that people have had in mind. After all, nobody thinks it offends equality to send some people to jail and not others—even though such treatment on the part of the state could hardly be more disparate—because there is an important difference in a just legal system between the sheep and the goats—namely, that the goats have been found guilty of a crime. The reason this does not offend equality, of course, is that there is an ethically relevant distinction between the As and the Bs here. And I have always drawn the inference from such cases that the key to equality is best understood negatively: Equality as a social ideal is a matter of not taking irrelevant distinctions into account. All the work here will go into deciding what distinctions are relevant. But in my judgment that is exactly where the work *should* go.

To understand equality this way is to see it as requiring that we treat like cases alike and thus to consider what makes two people or two kinds of people morally alike for current purposes. People should be treated differently because there are *grounds* for treating them differently (or at least no grounds for not doing so): Egalitarians are

---

5. I do not think Post makes these conflations, but I think he could have done more to draw attention to the muddles to which I try to draw attention.

6. *United Steelworkers of America v. Weber*, 443 U.S. 193 (1979).

7. *See* John Stuart Mill, *The Subjection of Women* (Susan Moller Okin ed., Hackett Pub. Co. 1988) (1869).

people who have strong views about which grounds are permissible (and impermissible). You might think that social identities — race, ethnicity, gender, class, sexuality, religious affiliation — are never proper grounds for disparate treatment; you might think, like some of the good burghers of Santa Cruz, that (at least when we are acting as employers and public officials) we ought not to treat the fat differently from the skinny or the pretty from the plain. I used to think something like this myself, so I would not regard you as foolish if you did. But I no longer think that so general a proscription can be right.

And that is because of another important feature of equality as a social ideal; namely, that questions of equality largely arise when the treatment is not only disparate but in some way invidiously so. It is one thing to give pink cookies to the girls and blue ones to the boys, but another to give the boys expensive toys and the girls cheap trinkets. There are those who think we should never treat females and males differently as such — that is, that our ground for treating them differently should never be that they are men and women. I confess to thinking that such gender blindness would be slightly crazy or, in our world at least, simply impossible.[8] Sexuality, as it is currently configured, makes the distinction between males and females relevant for most people: Is it really wrong to pay more attention to the men than the women at the party, if I am on the lookout for a partner? Gender (and it *is* gender, not just sex) seems relevant — or at least seems so for most people. As I scan the party, what I am considering offering to a potential partner is not something that is invidious to offer only to someone who, for some reason and in some way, attracts me.[9] There are perfectly possible criticisms of the structure of sexual desire: It seems wrong, for example, to be out looking for someone whom I will enjoy abusing, even if that is what turns me on. But I do not think it can be wrong to

8. Post shares my skepticism about ignoring gender, of course. For example, he says that people are not "context-free" in ordinary social life, Post, p. 21, and he later observes that "sexual attraction is so firmly attached to existing gender roles that the effort to transform [them] . . . seems an implausible ambition for the law." See p. 30. ("Implausible" is, I think, an understatement.)

9. This is why Desperate, who writes to Miss Lonelyhearts, does not have a moral argument against those who fail to be sexually attracted to her. *See* p. 8.

be out looking for a man, or for a woman, as such. (This, by the way, immediately makes gender and race different for the purposes of thinking about disparate treatment, because there seems to be no morally acceptable feature of human life that stands to racial identity as sexuality stands to gender. That is one of the reasons why, as Post rightly observes, "antidiscrimination law seeks to exercise a far more sweeping transformation of race than of gender.")[10]

I am using *invidious* here as a term of art, to describe treatment that differentially affects A and B with the aim or effect of producing a result that disadvantages one or the other of them in virtue of her identity. So it is not enough that the outcome be disparate and to the disadvantage of one of them: It must be disparate because, in some sense, their identities are different.

Whether or not I am right about either of my points—that equality is not identity and that the ideal of equality is aimed at invidiously disparate treatment—Post, in his sociological account of American antidiscrimination law, agrees with me. It used to be taken for granted that it was all right for the state and for private employers and those who provided public accommodations to make invidious distinctions between blacks and whites and between men and women. That is, it used to be thought to be all right to give as a reason for granting something to A that you denied to B—a job, access to a hotel, voting rights—that A was white or male and B was black or female. The statutes and the constitutional law making of the last thirty or more years include many attempts to move away from that practice and that assumption.

Post's paper focuses on antidiscrimination as a principle in the laws regulating employment. But invidious disparate treatment occurs in many areas of social life, and it will be helpful, I think, to frame the issues he considers within a more general understanding. So let me define a category of what I shall call public actions. This is intended to cover actions taken by state officials in their official capacity—which are clearly subject to norms of nondiscrimination—but also to include actions undertaken by people in the course of hiring and managing em-

10. *See* p. 48.

ployees and in admitting people to and ministering to them in public accommodations. It is an interesting question why, in a liberal society, antidiscrimination should be enforced as a legal norm in the sphere of public actions that are not state actions. I think the answer is clear enough: In our world, allowing each of us a fair chance at developing a dignified, autonomous existence, in which we can pursue a life governed by aims and an identity that we have reflectively appropriated, requires that we have access to employment and public space, as well as to the rights and privileges of the citizen. Dignity and autonomy being the core liberal values, a liberal will want the state to insist on reasonable access to employment and to public space for all. Why limit this insistence to public actions? Because to include other spheres of action within the ambit of antidiscrimination law — to require me not to distinguish between men and women, blacks and whites, in my everyday interactions — would infringe on my capacity to construct my own life. Freedom of expression and of association are central to such self-construction, and requiring me to have dinner parties in which gender or racial identity does not feature as a ground for choosing the guests interferes with these freedoms.

Because liberals believe not just in dignity but in equal dignity, what is made available by the state should be made available equally to everyone. The invocation of equality here must mean that the rights in question should not be denied to anyone by virtue of a feature that is morally irrelevant in the context. And so here, in the crafting of these regulations, there is space for discussion of which features should and should not be taken into account.

Post takes up exactly such a discussion when he distinguishes *Wilson*[11] and *Fesel*,[12] suggesting that gender is relevant in the context of sexual privacy but not in the context of the forms of service properly provided by airline staff.[13] I agree that this is the right sort of way to make the distinction between these cases. But we cannot always say simply that gender is relevant to employment in the context of sexual

_____ 11. *Wilson v. Southwest Airlines Co.*, 517 F. Supp. 292 (N.D. Tex. 1981).

12. *Fessel v. Masonic Home of Delaware, Inc.*, 447 F. Supp. 1346 (D. Del. 1978).

13. *See* pp. 33–34.

privacy, because we should then have to hold that *Griffin*[14] was wrongly decided. In that case what mattered was the relative weight of the sexual privacy rights of prisoners on the one hand, and the righs of women to equal treatment as prison guards on the other.[15] Prisoners do have sexual privacy rights (it would be wrong to broadcast photographs of showering prisoners for the gratification of the general public). The gender of prison guards is, indeed, therefore not irrelevant. But, in this context, sexual privacy weighs less than the need to open to women on the same terms as men forms of employment previously closed to them. The general point is that we may have to consider sometimes not just whether gender is relevant but also how weighty a consideration it provides.

I shall call the rights granted to us by laws that regulate public actions "public rights," and those that limit only actions taken by the state I shall refer to, in the usual way, as civil rights. Constraining employers, hotelkeepers, and the like by granting us public rights against them does indeed limit their freedom, but it does so in a way that is usually less central to their life projects than the opportunities they would deny us are to ours. (That is why the limitation to public actions is appropriate, though there is reasonable room for debate about exactly what belongs in the category of public action.) Where constraining an employer to grant us public rights does interfere profoundly with individual or collective projects—as requiring the Catholic Church to employ women as priests undoubtedly would—we cannot justify it on these grounds. And, since we must, as a result, adjudicate the claims of individuals against such organizations, we are speaking here of the balancing of opposing interests.

It would be a mistake to allow the centrality of a project to my individuality by itself to trump your interests in such cases: Do we want the centrality of anti-Semitic hatred to my life to entitle me to keep Jews out of my hotel, for example? And so, we are obliged also, in the end, to address the merits of the projects.

In attempting to avoid invidious discrimination in public actions on

14. *Griffin v. Michigan Dep't of Corrections*, 654 F. Supp. 690 (E.D. Mich. 1982).
15. *See* pp. 35–36.

the grounds of gender or race, we discover at once that it is not enough simply to require that race and gender not figure in the announced reasoning of public actors. People and legislators can easily cover gender bias by pretending that it is really something else—long hair, earrings, the risk of motherhood—that they are worried about. That intentions are easy to disguise means that we have a reason to look beyond facial neutrality and see whether there is not an invidious hidden agenda. But there is a deeper reason than this why we must look beyond facial neutrality. The fundamental rationale that I sketched for public rights was that they provide opportunities for their beneficiaries that are essential to a dignified autonomous life: If an action deprives me of such an opportunity, it hardly matters, from this point of view, that this was not the result of intentional malice. Of course, it may be that the deprivation was by virtue of a morally relevant feature. (For example, I might have been deprived of my liberty because I committed a crime.) Thus, it is important in assessing the harm done to me by the deprivation of an opportunity that we ask whether it can be justified. But if it cannot, then, so it seems to me, the fact that the agents of my deprivation did not intend to harm me seems less important than that they did in fact harm me. I may be entitled to a remedy, even if they are not reasonably to be subjected to punishment.

That, in my view, is why antidiscrimination law naturally leads to discussion of "disparate impact." It is also why something like a "bona fide occupational qualification" (BFOQ) exception seems natural as well: If my gender, nationality, or racial identity are in fact relevant for the purposes of a public action, then there is nothing morally troublesome about taking them into account. (So we ought to admit the possibility of a BFOQ in the case of race, as the federal law does not, because there seems nothing harmful, in a realist production, in requiring that we have actors who look—and sound—like people of whatever racial identity they are representing.)

I have been doing what philosophers often do, namely, developing a general picture of the normative constraints on a social practice—in this case the legal granting of public rights against discrimination on grounds of gender and race—without taking much notice of actually existing practice. But I need this much by way of background to raise the two lines of discussion that I would like to raise about the claims Post makes in his lecture. Both of the lines I want to pursue are, I hope, in the spirit of friendly amendments; but the only way I know to think through what I believe about such things is from the sort of first principles I have been sketching.

The first line of discussion has to do with the promiscuous use of the word *stereotype* in the judgments that Post quotes and discusses. In my view, this word is being asked to do too much work, and that has led to confusion. On the basis of the examples that Post cites, it seems to me that *stereotype* in American antidiscrimination law covers at least three distinct ideas.

The first is the idea of ascribing to an individual a property in the belief that it is characteristic of some social group to which she belongs, where there is indeed a statistical correlation between that property and being a member of that group, but where, in fact, she does not have that property. This is the case of the strong woman, "Mary," who presents herself for a job as a firefighter and is told that she will not be considered because "women are not strong enough to be firemen." Here, there is a general fact about the group that is relevant to the employment decision: Strength, let us suppose, really is a BFOQ for a firefighter, and women really are, on average, weaker than men. But this general fact does not bear on the question of Mary's suitability for the job if she is in fact stronger than most men—stronger, in fact, than the weakest male fireman. Let's call these statistical stereotypes.

Public action toward an individual based on a statistical stereotype when she is, in fact, atypical of her group, burdens her for no good reason. The economically minded will object that, given the statistical fact, there may be higher search costs in filling positions if you have to consider even members of groups who are characteristically not suitable for them than there would be if you were allowed to rule them out in advance. If the costs were astronomically higher or if they somehow burdened some employers more than others—for example, if much of their competition was from companies working in regimes without antidiscrimination law—then there might, indeed, be a cause for subsidy here. But there seems no good reason why the costs to the business should trump the costs to the qualified but unrepresentative member of her group. Rights, whether public in general or civil in particular, always have costs, and they are not always borne by the state. It strikes me as a fortiori true that the cost to business should not trump the cost to the potential employee if the fact that there are few qualified members of the group is the result of historical injustice or present discrimination. Post isolates this issue in his discussion of the "paradigmatic example" of a "refusal to grant a BFOQ exemption to an employer who claims that women should not be hired for particular positions because 'the arduous nature of the work-related activity renders women physically unsuited for the jobs.'"[16] But, as I suggested at the start, I think it would be helpful to point out how different statistical stereotypes and the issues they raise are from some other uses of the term *stereotype* in the case law, two of which I discuss immediately below.

A second idea invoked by the word *stereotype* is just a false belief about a group. In the context of antidiscrimination, the relevance of such stereotypes—let's call them simply false stereotypes—is that a public actor may give as her ground for doing something the belief that A has some characteristic, because she believes that all members of a group to which A belongs, have, or are very likely to have, that characteristic. And she may do this even when the characteristic is not, in fact, common in the group. The classic examples here are ethnic stereotypes, which lead people, say, not to do business with members of a group because they are purportedly shifty and dishonest, when, in fact, they are not, or at any rate not more so than anybody else. Simply false stereotypes burden people for no good reason, too. But to identify the burden may require an inquiry into the question whether the stereotype is in fact simply false.

The third and, in my view, most interesting sense of the word *stereotype* comes up in the case of gender in relation to the discussion of norms of dress and behavior. Here a stereotype is not a view about how members of the group behave *simpliciter:* It is grounded in a social consensus about how they *ought* to behave to conform appropriately to the norms associated with membership in their group. I shall call this a nor-

16. *See* p. 24.

mative stereotype. When employers require female employees to wear dresses and male employees not to do so, they are invoking normative gender stereotypes.

It is perhaps worth observing that there are obvious connections between statistical and normative stereotypes. Many of the generalizations involved in statistical stereotyping are true because there are normative stereotypes to which people are conforming.

Now granting these distinctions, we can see that different kinds of stereotypes deserve different responses. Both the first and the second kinds of stereotypes involve intellectual error — either misunderstanding the facts, in the case of simply false stereotypes, or misunderstanding their relevance, in the case of statistical ones. But there is no reason to suppose that normative stereotypes as such must be wrong, or that public actions grounded on them are to be criticized, even where they involve differences in treatment that are judged to be invidious. For example, given the way the clothing market works, the demand made of a woman that she wear business attire appropriate to her sex may well require her to spend more money than the same demand made of her male colleagues. That makes it invidious, in my term-of-art sense, because she is paying a cost by virtue of her gender. But it is at least not obvious to me that this is a harm that rises to the level of requiring a public right, or the expenditure of public funds, to remedy it.

We can now revisit a few of the cases Post discusses with these distinctions in mind. Begin with the Santa Cruz ordinance. Those who favored it, Post says, did so because they thought that employment and housing decisions ought not to depend on an "irrelevant characteristic" and that "decisions based upon appearance so often merely express 'simple bigotry.' " [17] A characteristic is irrelevant to whether or not someone will be a good employee if it gives no indication of his capacity to do the job, and it is irrelevant to whether or not he will be a good tenant if it gives no indication as to whether he will be clean and quiet and pay his rent on time. Here the defenders were arguing that appearance invoked simply false stereotypes. They might also have argued that statistical stereotyping was a danger and that the ordinance

17. *See* p. 4.

would encourage employers and landlords to take special care to examine whether people whose appearances they disliked would actually
be good employees or tenants. The suggestion that trying to "control
the look of their workforce"[18] echoed the mentality that led to anti-
black discrimination in housing and employment suggests, however,
that they might also have had normative stereotypes in mind. In particular, in relation to dress and self-chosen aspects of appearance, it
might be that what they were objecting to was the attempt to enforce
norms in areas that properly should be under the control of the individual. These strike me as arguments worth considering — and as better
arguments than those suggested by the idea that equality requires either
sameness or blindness to difference.

But I think the heart of their argument had very little to do with
stereotyping, even though it seems to have been invoked a good deal
in the discussion. For the real argument about discrimination in the
area of appearance was that what employers and landlords were doing
was expressing their distaste for or discomfort with people whom they
found in various ways unattractive: obese people, people with an eccen-
tric sense of dress or bodily adornment, and the like.[19] What is wrong
with this is that it places a burden on people either in respect of a
characteristic over which they have no control (ugliness, say) or over
which they are entitled to maintain control themselves; for those characteristics that I ought to be entitled to regulate myself, the threat of
being fired or being unable to find a place to live is illegitimately coercive.[20] The problem is not stereotyping but bigotry — that is, unjus-

18. *Id.* (quoting Stephen G. Hirsch, "Santa Cruz Law Could Be Attacked for Vagueness;
Proposed Ordinance Would Bar Bias Based on Appearance," *The Recorder*, Jan. 17, 1992,
at 1).

19. *See* pp. 6–7.

20. I am here taking up Post's suggestion, in his discussion of the Santa Cruz ordinance,
that discrimination on the basis of appearance threatens autonomy. *See* pp. 6–7. But I
do not accept the idea that Post suspects may underlie "legal judgments of unfairness,"
namely, that it depends on "whether a stigmatizing attribute is . . . somehow essential or
integral to a person, like their religion." See p. 11. For the range of considerations that it
seems proper to exclude in distinguishing people in a certain context may include characteristics that are mutable and important (like religion), mutable and unimportant
(like hair color), immutable and unimportant (like eye color — at least for the moment),

tified hatred or contempt. (I do not deny that there are connections between stereotyping and bigotry: Bigotry often leads to stereotyping and stereotyping can lead to bigotry. But each can stand alone.)

In the passages of judicial interpretation of Title VII that Post cites toward the beginning of his discussion of the Federal Civil Rights Act of 1964, there is some mention of stereotypes, but the primary focus is not on normative stereotypes.[21] The Court speaks of "stubborn but irrational prejudice" in *Lam v. University of Hawaii*,[22] suggesting that it is cognitive problems—simply false or statistical stereotyping—that are at issue. In *Donohue v. Shoe Corp. of America*,[23] there is explicit mention of forming "opinions of people on the basis of skin color, religion, national origin, . . . and other superficial features." Similarly, in the ensuing discussion of state antidiscrimination statutes, there is talk of "stereotyped impressions about the characteristics of a class to which the person belongs," which could also mean either that the characteristics are incorrectly assigned to the class (simply false stereotyping) or to the individual (statistical stereotyping).[24]

But there are hints all along that normative stereotyping is also in the offing. When Justice Brennan in *Price Waterhouse v. Hopkins*[25] interprets federal law as insisting that "sex, race, religion, and national origin are not relevant to the selection, evaluation, or compensation of employees," he must mean that they are not relevant *in se*, because they are clearly relevant statistically. To say that they are irrelevant *in se* might seem to be to reject normative stereotypes that declare certain jobs suitable or unsuitable for African Americans or for women.

---

immutable and important (like race—as normally understood). Most people I know would find it unfair to deny a job to someone because their eyes were blue, their hair was dyed red, or they were Catholic or Asian, at least in the absence of some connection between these properties and the nature of the task. (Post does not, of course, endorse the view he here ascribes to the legal mind: It is possible that he, too, shares my sense that it is mistaken.)

21. *See* pp. 12–13.

22. 40 F.3d 1551, 1563 (9th Cir. 1994).

23. 337 F. Supp. 1357, 1359 (C.D. Cal. 1972).

24. *See* p. 13 (citing *Miller v. C.A. Muer Corp.*, 420 Mich. 355, 362–63 [1984]).

25. 490 U.S. 228, 239 (1989) (Brennan, J., plurality opinion).

Someone who neither invalidly invokes statistical stereotyping to mis-assess an individual nor wrongly characterizes the abilities of women or African Americans might nonetheless believe that each has a proper place that is different from the place of men or of white people.

Thus, I am not inclined to accept Post's account of stereotypes as "the conventions that underwrite the social practices of gender."[26] For that suggests that stereotypes are reducible to normative stereotypes. Nevertheless, this is, in essence, something of a semantic disagreement, because he does in fact distinguish between stereotypes in his sense and questions concerning the relevance of statistical generalizations about classes of people to the treatment of individuals in those classes.

The importance of normative stereotypes — which I have elsewhere called scripts for identities[27] — is central to understanding the place of identity in moral and civic life. I do not have time now to explore the question why it is that social identities are so crucial for our individualities. But if, as liberals at least since John Stuart Mill have proposed, the construction of one's own individuality, the creation of a self, is indeed a project for every human life, and if, as much recent multicultural and feminist discussion has made plain, collective identities are a resource for that self-creation and not just a hindrance, then it follows that we must accept the existence of normative stereotypes. For a social identity is, among other things, a set of normative scripts for shaping your behavior, your plans, your life. If this is right, however, not just any normative stereotypes will do. They have to be configured in such a way as to serve as potential instruments in the construction of a dignified individuality. To the extent that existing norms, enforced through public action, construct an identity as lacking in dignity, or have built into them the inferiorization of those who bear it, they are not such instruments. I think Post is entirely right, then, to insist that what matters in antidiscrimination law is the reshaping of gender norms, not their abolition. The abolition of gender norms, as I say, would be the abolition of gender and the radical reformulation — perhaps beyond human

26. See p. 23.

27. *See* K. Anthony Appiah, "Identity, Authenticity, Survival: Multicultural Societies and Social Reproduction," in *Multiculturalism: Examining "The Politics of Recognition"* 149–63 (Amy Gutmann ed., 1994).

recognition—of sexuality. But their reform could begin to make it less true that our society constructs women as inferior to men.

It is an interesting question what we should say about racial identities here. If identifying as an African American (the socially constructed identity, not some putative biological race) is a source of value in the shaping of the modern identities of at least some Americans of African ancestry, then it seems to me that we must accept that at least some normative stereotypes—about dress or speech or participation in Kwanza, for example—have value. But it would still be open to us to say that, although such normative stereotypes do indeed have value, their value does not make them a suitable basis for invidiously different treatment in the sphere of what I have called public actions. I doubt myself that this is right, at least at the moment. For to say that would be to require that there be no public acts that disadvantaged members of any racial group. And, as Post rightly points out,[28] that would rule out any form of affirmative action in relation to race.

This last claim is controversial because some deny that affirmative action for racial minorities disadvantages white people by virtue of their race. It is a coherent position that advantaging a Latina in a competition for a job or a place at a university does not deprive any white person of anything, because the job or the place was not something to which he was entitled. However, I prefer to accept that in affirmative action there are winners and losers, but that there is sometimes a justification for the practice nevertheless.

Post rightly remarks that the "law seeks . . . a far more sweeping transformation of race than of gender."[29] I think that the exploration of the ways in which collective identities serve to shape lives positively as well as negatively might lead the law—or, at any rate, some of its practitioners—to be more tolerant of the idea that racial identities can be a proper basis for distinguishing between people.

The final line of thought I want to take up briefly is also relevant to thinking about affirmative action. Once we accept Post's picture of

28. *See* pp. 50–57.
29. *See* p. 48.

American antidiscrimination law, judges and legislatures and citizens must take up the question of which forms of invidiously disparate public action require remedy. We cannot prudently attempt to deal with all of them, making it a crime, for example, to be less courteous to black than to white guests at hotels. (If my experience in this country is anything to go by, this would be one of the easiest ways of increasing the white prison population.) I think there is an obvious way to focus such discussions. It is to ask how central that form of public action is to maintaining sexual or racial inequality. Because racism and sexism are systematic and patterned, not mere accidental agglomerations of individualized prejudices, this is a reasonable question. And I think that those judges who have found it unreasonable to require employers to allow men to wear their hair long,[30] for example, could rightly have given as their rationale the fact that such employer's preferences simply play too small a role in shaping gender in ways that disadvantage women. Similarly, requiring Morehouse to admit more white students strikes me as something that will not reduce racial inequality in America, while integrating the elite schools that had historically excluded black people certainly was an important step in that direction. I think this proposal also allows us to make a plausible distinction between *Wilson* (the case involving Southwest Airlines flight attendants)[31] and *Craft* (the case of the female TV news anchor).[32] Here we can say that the practice of offering airline service that is aimed at attracting heterosexual men of conventional tastes by requiring women to "act sexy" for them is demeaning to women and sustains male supremacy in a way or to a degree that requiring a woman news anchor to "maintain professional, businesslike appearances, 'consistent with community standards,'" does not.[33] In fact the standards invoked by the television station in *Craft* presuppose that women, though governed by different norms of dress, are nevertheless properly to be found in professional, business positions. I do not deny that the codes of dress for

30. *See* p. 36.
31. *Wilson v. Southwest Airlines Co.*, 517 F. Supp. 292 (N.D. Tex. 1981).
32. *Craft v. Metromedia, Inc.*, 766 F.2d 1205 (8th Cir. 1985).
33. *See* p. 31 (quoting *Craft*, 766 F.2d at 1209–10).

women in the "conservative" Kansas City market[34] are likely to play a role in limiting the opportunities of businesswomen or reflect a lack of equal respect for them. But they do so, I believe, to a significantly lesser degree than do the codes requiring airline attendants to engage in "sexy dressing."

My proposal is, of course, a proposal about one of the issues that should be taken up by courts in deciding how to reshape gender and race in America: It is a proposal that could be taken up only by a court that had already grasped the sociological account of antidiscrimination law articulated by Post. So I would hope that the elegance of his arguments will persuade not just me but some of those public actors who have to construct and administer American antidiscrimination law.

34. *See* p. 31.

Judith Butler | "Appearances Aside"

Robert Post's essay is, at one level, an inquiry into recent legal efforts to ban discrimination on the basis of appearance. He surveys various appearance codes and distinguishes them as a specifically new set of instances of antidiscrimination regulation. His paper begins with these examples, but quickly moves to a broader consideration of the implicit conception of the person, the person as he or she becomes subject to the law and, specifically, as a being against whom discrimination can occur. If how a person appears is central to who the person is, and if the person ought to have a right to have protected what is most central to the person, then it follows that the appearance of the person ought to be protected against discrimination. If, however, the person against whom discrimination on the basis of appearance occurs is one who is separable from the way in which he or she appears, then it seems crucial to understand whether appearance is central to the concept of the person at work in these laws and regulations. If it should prove to be the case that a person has value and ought to be treated on the basis of that value, apart from the way in which that person appears, and we base our antidiscrimination claims on this proposition, then it seems that the person is not centrally defined by his or her appearance. Obviously, the second argument is not compatible with the first, at least not on any manifest level. So the question becomes: How did antidiscrimination law arrive at this plateau in which the implicit concept of the person whose value the law seeks to protect is fundamentally at odds with itself? The person is and is not, centrally, his or her appearance. Where can one go from here?

Post's essay sketches out the notion of the person as fundamentally defined by his or her appearance as the sociological view, one which holds that the concrete, social ways in which persons appear in the world are central to their value and meaning as persons.[1] The paper also offers as an example of a "transcendental" position the concept of the person as having value in spite of any and all ways of appearing in the world.[2] Post then asks us to resist the transcendental seductions of antidiscrimination law, develop a skepticism toward the conception of the person that disavows his or her social mode of appearing, and embrace instead a sociological approach that avows appearance as central to personhood.[3]

What is the transcendental seduction to which he refers? According to the transcendental view as Post relates it, a person has an intrinsic worth or an instrumental value that is not reducible to or decipherable from the various ways in which persons appear.[4] On the basis of the transcendental view of personhood, a few prescriptive guidelines follow. First, we are asked *not* to take into account a person's appearance in making employment decisions. To obey or implement such a law, however, we need to know how it is that we can *not* take appearance into account. Does this mean that when we consider a person, we do not consider the visible features of that person? Is it really possible not to consider such features if they are precisely, definitionally, what appear, especially in, for example, an interview situation? How do we consider such a person without taking into consideration what we see, or are we being asked to look at a person without actually seeing what

1. *See* Robert Post, "Prejudicial Appearances: The Logic of American Antidiscrimination Law," reproduced in this volume, pp. 1–53, see pp. 19–20, 40.
2. *See* pp. 10–21.
3. *See* pp. 21–53.
4. *See* pp. 10–21.

we see, engaging in a practice of disavowal? Are either of these strategies of compliance practicable?

Post suggests that the transcendental conception of antidiscrimination law assumes that we *can* separate a person from the way in which the person appears, and that the separability of the person from his or her appearance presumes the person has an ontological status that preexists any appearance. Moreover, this person has an ontological status that preexists any social status as well. What is it we are supposed to consider, then, about this person who preexists his or her appearance? How do we "see" or find these salient, nonvisible attributes? A judge considering a claim of discrimination might consider how this person has been treated and make a judgment on that matter by seeking recourse to a normative conception of the essential worth of the person, a worth that would be, in line with egalitarian principle, the same as any other person's worth, a worth that pertains to persons as such. Or a judge might consider whether a person can perform a job well, and so try to make a judgment about the person's technical skill. This hypothetical person is thus either a Kantian soul with deontological value whose intrinsic worth is never fully expressed in any appearance, social or otherwise, or the person is reducible to an instrumental capacity, at which point the person is understood as an analogical relation to a set of functions.[5]

Post warns us against accepting either or both of these conceptions of the person that seek to establish the extraneous relation of appearance to personhood. Although Post argues that the dominant legal conception presumes "a correspondence between pre-social individuals . . . and 'context-free' functional capacities,"[6] it seems like no easy task to reconcile the Kantian and functionalist paradigms. The Kantian paradigm is often used as a critique of the functionalist one in arguments that claim that the functionalist model discounts the deontological worth of persons. The functionalist, on the other hand, more often than not tends to mock the speculative status of the Kantian assertion, counterarguing that a person is nothing other than what a person can

5. For an introduction to deontological and instrumentalist ethics, see Paul W. Taylor, *Problems of Moral Philosophy* (1972).

6. *See* p. 39.

do, thereby collapsing ontology into capacity. Of course, what constitutes "capacity" may be equally as speculative as the "intrinsic worth" of persons, but the functionalists tend to presume the verifiability of the assessment of skills, relying on tests or observation or both. In fact, to the extent that the functionalist relies on observation or, indeed, that a means of testing skills has an observational component, the functionalist approach also depends for its conclusion on how people appear to those who are judging their capacities. In this sense, the functionalist position does not remain fully distinct from the position that asserts that personhood requires appearance.

Indeed, these functionalist and transcendental conceptions might be understood to constitute something like a modern antinomy of pre-social and disembodied conceptions of personhood, both of which try to determine the person prior to appearance, but which determine the person in differing, if not opposing ways, either in terms of intrinsic worth or presumed instrumental values. Both might be understood to be perspectives on persons that have developed in response to modern forms of rationalization.[7] The deontological seeks to resist rationalization by insisting that persons must be treated as ends, and not means;[8] the functionalist might be said to give a certain moral rationale to the processes of functional rationalization, disembedding individuals from traditional contexts, and shifting the legal focus from the status of individuals to the tasks that they perform.

Post wants us to reject these notions because they both seek, with varying degrees of success, to deny what is undeniable about persons, namely, their status as social beings. One might speculate here that the debate about the moral pros and cons of rationalization have occluded the importance of the social constitution of persons. In other words, Post is asking us to sidestep this particular set of options and to consider instead the way in which antidiscrimination law ought to presuppose the person not only as one who is, by definition, *engaged in* a set

---

7. For an explanation of rationalization, see Max Weber, *The Theory of Social and Economic Organization* 23 (Talcott Parsons ed., A. M. Henderson and Talcott Parsons trans., Oxford Univ. Press 1947).

8. *See* Immanuel Kant, The Moral Law: Kant's Groundwork of the Metaphysic of Morals 74–77 (H. J. Paton trans., Hutchinson and Co. 1948).

of social practices, but one who might be said *to be* a social practice, one whose ontology is that of an ongoing and revisable social practice or set of social practices. Note that this would be different from saying that there is a person who engages in social practices, for the former "person" in such an instance might well be engaged in something else, and the practice is grammatically positioned as extraneous to the person. To claim that what a person "is" is constituted by the practices in which he or she engages is to claim that the person is a mode or a set of modes of socially engaged practices. No practice, no person.

One might simply counterpose the transcendental and social conceptions of personhood and argue that the social is better, that it is more fully descriptive, that it takes into account the world as we know it. But does the distinction between the transcendental and the social finally hold? Is the transcendental always compromised by the dimension of social reality it seeks to exclude? Would it not be a stronger argument to claim that personhood presupposes its social ontology, and that no transcendental or functionalist position can work without making this very social presumption? Whereas I cannot fully elaborate that argument here, I do think that there is a very strong argument in Post's reading that is worth pursuing. That argument runs somewhat as follows: (1) If certain codes and statutes ask us not to discriminate on the basis of appearance, and (2) these codes and statutes hold that what we judge to be relevant about a person when we consider employing that person, for instance, ought not to include aspects of appearance that neither have bearing on the tasks a person can perform nor constitute an essential feature of that person, it follows that these codes and statutes presume the ontological integrity of a person prior to appearance. But this conclusion raises a serious question: Is there a person apart from his or her appearance? If we insist in return that surely there are dimensions to a person that are legally relevant to discrimination cases and that do not strictly speaking "appear," we still have not answered the question of whether a person can be observed or judged on whatever basis without first appearing. This is simply to say that appearance provides the epistemological condition for judging another person's worth or skill, even if that worth or skill is not, as it often is not, reducible to appearance itself. Thus, if appearance is the way in which persons are made available to judgment (which is not to say that all we can judge of a person is his or her appearance), then what is it we purport to judge when we judge a person? Do we judge something that exists, or does our judgment bring into being its own presumption about personhood, operating performatively, as it were, to install its speculative premise as human reality?

I do not take Post to be making the sweeping claim that persons are nothing but their appearance, a form of social phenomenalism. Although he does not pursue the issue here, it would be interesting to know how he accounts for those dimensions of personhood that do not, strictly speaking, appear: dimensions of psychic life that remain unexpressed or inexpressible, dimensions of human biology that for the most part remain concealed, aspects of human experience, especially those pertaining to time, such as memory or expectation, that cannot appear in any direct form in the present. Indeed, we can surely find myriad antidiscrimination claims made on behalf of these nonapparent dimensions of life, claims made on the basis of personal integrity, cultural history, or memory, all of which assert nonphenomenal aspects of personhood. Certainly there are dimensions of psychic and biological life that have only an oblique relation to appearance, and there are probably characteristics of persons, even those that are relevant to the question of job performance, that do not appear in any visual sense. If the meaning of persons is, in Post's view, *not* fully exhausted in the realm of appearance, it would be good to know how we can continue to conceive of persons as social beings without, as it were, reducing them to the ways in which they appear.

Post's argument relies on there being a crucial connection between a notion of persons conceived as social beings and one in which persons exist in an essential relation to appearance. I take Post to be arguing that certain social categories, such as sex and race, are fundamental to social reality as we live it, and that they are essential coordinates within the social field, ones which, at this point in time and culture, are essential to the social meaning of personhood. Moreover, these are categories that appear, and they depend on appearance for their social legibility. I would add: Some modes of appearance for these categories are "marked" and some are "unmarked," which means that some stand out, such as blackness, as visible social signs, whereas whiteness, which is no less social, is nevertheless part of the taken-for-granted visual field, a sign of its presumptive hegemony. These categories and the differential relations among them structure the culturally lived horizons of appearance: They determine the visual field in which we live, one that is saturated with social meaning.

What does this mean for the problem of judgment as it is raised in Post's paper? In our everyday practice, we do notice, and it does make a difference whether someone is understood to be of a given gender or transsexual or in transition, or whether someone is of a given race or of mixed race inheritance and/or racially indeterminate. I gather that Post would also say that the way in which these categories matter is not always in the service of discriminatory aims.[9] But as conventional sites for discrimination, this will be part of the meaning they bear in the social world in which we live.

There are, of course, those who would say that to notice such categories is already to have discriminated, but I take it that this is not Post's view and that he would maintain a social operation of such categories that is not necessarily discriminatory in its aims. But he does tend to conflate the social category of gender, for instance, with its stereotypical norms. He writes, for example, that the "generalizations and stereotypes" on which gender discrimination relies are coextensive with the practice of gender itself,[10] which would suggest that any and all references to gender are potentially or actually discriminatory. Such "stereotypes," he writes, "are, of course, the conventions that underwrite the social practice of gender. To eliminate all such generalizations and stereotypes would be to eliminate the practice."[11] Post goes on to

---

9. Anthony Appiah has argued that racial categories always work in the service of discriminatory aims. He writes, "The truth is that there are no races: there is nothing in the world that can do all we ask 'race' to do for us," and proceeds to refer to the "evil of the concept." *See* Anthony Appiah, "The Uncompleted Argument: Du Bois and the Illusion of Race," in *"Race", Writing, and Difference* 35–36 (Henry Louis Gates Jr., ed., 1985). For a similar argument, see Sandra Harding, *Whose Science? Whose Knowledge?: Thinking from Women's Lives* (1991).

10. *See* p. 23.

11. *Id.*

worry that the main aim of antidiscrimination law is to "disestablish the category of sex and to replace it with the imperatives of functional rationality."[12] But is the practice of gender exhausted by the operation of the stereotype, or is there a dimension of gender that is not only antistereotypical, which would still be tied to the stereotype, but *a*stereotypical, which would be free of the stereotype or, perhaps, in a relation of indifference to it? How do we account for the transformation of the stereotype within the practice of gender if there were not something else in gender, as it were, that is not immediately coopted or foreclosed by the stereotype? Of course, it is a major social and political question whether gender should be eliminated as a category and, if so, what might be the most practical means to effect that solution. But it is not clear that the elimination of gender is an undisputed political goal of feminism. Indeed, given the spate of feminist work on transforming gender, of relieving it of its entrenched hierarchies, of producing new cultural forms of gender, it is unclear whether the practice of gender is, or must be, coextensive with its stereotype. Indeed, those who suffer specific forms of gender discrimination make claims before the law that it is precisely the nonstereotypical expression of gender that provides the occasion for discriminatory conduct.[13] Thus, such claims implicitly refute the more rigid feminist thesis that gender stereotypes underwrite gender, a formulation that cannot countenance the existing deviations from the norm.[14] Even if the stereotype were eliminated, would that be the end of gender? Would that elimination perhaps only constitute the end of gender as we have known it, and the beginning of gender as a social practice governed by a transformed—and transformable—set of social norms?

What I take Post to claim is that if we are obliged by the transcendental and functionalist imperatives in the law to ignore the realm of appearance in questions of employment, admissions, and the allocation of resources, we ignore the very condition—appearance—that allows persons to matter to us. In other words, if race and gender are central

12. *Id.* at p. 24.
13. *See, e.g.*, Katherine M. Franke, "What's Wrong with Sexual Harassment?", 49 *Stan L. Rev.* 691 (1997).
14. *See, e.g.*, Catharine MacKinnon, *Toward a Feminist Theory of the State* 126–54 (1989).

to how we come to understand other people, and if those categories establish, to some degree, the conditions under which persons appear, and how they appear (sometimes even "whether" they appear) as persons, can we then even have a notion of the person if we are asked to discount the realm of appearance?

Let me make this point yet another way: We could say that gender and race are attributes of a person and that if we do not consider those attributes, the personhood of the person is still intact: "This is Peter; he happens to be x, y, and z." But what happens if we consider these categories not as simple attributes but as social conditions of appearance and intelligibility? If our very notion of personhood is dependent on such social categories, indeed if we cannot have a conception of a person without first determining that person's sex, for instance, then it seems that the elimination of the category eliminates the person as well. I take it that the constitutive power of these social categories is what Post has in mind, authorizing, I hope, my formulation that a person is the social practice of gender or, indeed, is the social practice of race (where the copula is understood to resist a reduction to the categories at hand). In matters of race, this argument becomes more complex, and, finally, it is complex for sex as well. A mixed race person may be precisely one whose "race" is not identifiable on the basis of appearance, or one for whom the category of race has become finally undecidable. Similarly, a person with complex chromosomal arrangements or a transitional transsexual will be one for whom sex is not precisely a stable or systematic social category. We might say, though, that their asystematic appearance in such cases is precisely understandable over and against the norms that are stable and systematic. This would all be well and good, but if the social aim at hand here is the transformation of such norms, the unstable and asystematic operation of such categories must have a transformative effect on the norm itself, such that gender and race never get to be the same again.

I suppose this brings me to my one point of worry here. In claiming that race and gender are stable and systematic features of social reality and social appearance in particular, and in claiming that persons cannot legibly appear to us without these conditions of social appearance in place, are we perhaps fortifying these categories precisely in their stereotypicality and persistence? By what means, then, are they disrupted and revised?

Clearly Post looks to antidiscrimination law as a way to disrupt and transform such categories, and here I agree that this is indeed one very powerful instrument. But I wonder whether to achieve his goal of social transformation in the service of equality, he might need to revise his description of social reality. Post appears to understand these categories as pervasive and systematic in social reality: "We are," he writes, "socialized into a culture in which these differences matter, and matter in systematic ways." [15] There are, he writes, "social practices or norms within which categories like race, gender, and beauty acquire their significance," and these practices and norms are part of what constitute us as persons.[16] The law, Post writes, is also a social practice, one that is also steeped in these very norms and practices. Indeed, the law is made by those who participate in the above-mentioned social practices and who invariably replicate those norms. It follows from his view, then, that we ought not to idealize the law as a neutral instrument that might intervene in the social operation of such categories to eliminate them. Antidiscrimination law participates in the very practices it seeks to regulate; antidiscrimination law can become an instrument of discrimination in the sense that it must reiterate—and entrench—the stereotypical or discriminatory version of the social category it seeks to eliminate. Ideally, however, antidiscrimination law is a social practice that seeks to disrupt and transform another set of discriminatory social practices. Insofar as both are social practices, and society is underwritten by stereotype, it is hard to see that antidiscrimination law might transcend the stereotypes it seeks to eliminate.

If I am hiring someone, and I become mindful of antidiscrimination law, then I can find myself wondering how considerations of appearance fit into my assessment of the capabilities of a person. It may be that I do notice aspects of that person's appearance and decide that I will not countenance these features in making the employment decision I will make. Here it is not a matter of blinding myself to how the person

15. *See* p. 21.
16. *Id.*

appears but, rather, deciding what ought to count about that person for the job in question from within the observational realm in which that person appears. I take this to be a revised version of the practice of "blindness" that the transcendental turn asks us to make. Thus, it is *not* a question of blinding oneself to how a person appears, but a question instead of how the way in which a person appears blinds one to the worth and capability of the person. What if the way in which a person appears makes me wonder at some less than fully conscious level about the personhood of the person, of their worth and their capability as persons? Here it is not a question of setting aside one set of attributes to consider a person exclusive of those attributes, but a matter of unsettling the social conditions by which persons become intelligible at all.

For this challenge to take place, it must be possible for a person whose appearance calls the category of the person into question to enter into the field of appearance precisely as a person. This is the power the astereotypical has to rewrite the stereotype, the power that the asystematic and unstable in gender and race have to unsettle the epistemological conditions of human intelligibility, a power that is "had" to the extent that such a person is not first defeated by the powers of discrimination. The radical consequence of law, conceived as social practice, is to make us pause, and pause again, as we enter into the risky process of knowing and judging one another.

Thomas C. Grey | Cover Blindness

Robert Post's original and challenging essay starts with a puzzle: Why don't the champions of civil rights line up against "lookism" as they have against racism and sexism? The rhetoric of civil rights law denounces, in general and unqualified terms, discrimination based on stereotyping—which is to say, judging the worth of human beings on the basis of superficial characteristics like skin color. You can't judge a book by its cover, or so we say when we talk about race and gender. Does not the same principle make us say that beauty is only skin deep?

Yet even many ardent civil rights advocates share the intuition that using law to prohibit discrimination on the basis of appearance goes too far. Post thinks this intuition is no mere reflex of prejudice; he invokes it as the basis of a reductio against some standard assumptions of antidiscrimination law.

The maxim about books and their covers implies that a fair, meritocratic society looks beyond mere appearances and considers only the real person underneath when allocating important benefits and burdens. That would make discrimination against the physically ugly a paradigmatic form of bigotry. And if it is bigotry, it is not a trivial kind; studies show that less attractive people do tend to get fewer of the socially valued goods.[1] So why don't we rally around laws aimed to combat appearance discrimination?

Post wants to plant some doubts about the underlying "book and cover" distinction between mere appearance and underlying reality, with its implied notion that behind the facade lies a core (but often unapparent) "real individual," in whom all genuine merit resides. This concept, he argues, is too unhistorical, acontextual, and utopian — in a word, too abstract — to serve as a plausible underpinning for antidiscrimination law.[2] In the actual life-world, not only do we judge and get judged by appearances but it could not be otherwise — and that is why laws against appearance discrimination overreach even the most robust workable conception of equality under the law.

The more general point is that a contrast between mere physical appearance and true human reality does not provide a satisfactory basis even for the core of civil rights law, the prohibitions against race and gender discrimination.[3] We cannot live behind a veil effacing individuals' appearances as women or men, black, brown, or white. The social categories of race and gender are so much constituted by our conventional associations of appearance with identity that to disestablish those conventions across the board is beyond the law's capacity. If judges take seriously a rhetoric that purports to require this impossible degree of "cover blindness," they will invariably produce dishonest and misguided doctrine.

To replace the abstracted approach that is now dominant, Post proposes a "sociological" (that is, more contextual) conception of antidiscrimination law.[4] On this conception, the links between physical appearance and the status ascriptions we make when we identify someone by race or gender are not simply a set of harmful stereotypes, obstacles to individual liberation, to be extirpated by law insofar as possible. Rather, our conventions for attributing group identity to persons

1. See Robert Post, "Prejudicial Appearances: The Logic of American Antidiscrimination Law," reproduced in this volume, pp. 1–53.
2. See p. 9.
3. See pp. 2–21.
4. See pp. 21–39.

are embedded in social practices that partly constitute our very selves, collective and individual.

We pass antidiscrimination laws, then, not as steps in a campaign for the abolition of all stereotypes but with the humbler purpose of reforming undesirable aspects of the practices that mold our notions of ascriptive categories like gender and race. Those reforms are to be implemented through yet another set of embedded social practices: legislation, regulation, adjudication, and the informal dissemination of legal norms.

Post supports his critique and proposal mainly by reference to the law of gender discrimination, where the gap between the case law and the rhetoric of stereotype extirpation is particularly striking.[5] But his scattered references to the law of race, and particularly his praise of Justice Brennan's opinion in *United Steelworkers of America v. Weber*,[6] show how his argument applies throughout the domain of antidiscrimination law. The total extirpation of race as a significant identifying characteristic may be a conceivable goal, but any attempt to organize antidiscrimination law around such a utopian project is sure to distort the applicable legal doctrines.

I agree with the general thrust of Post's approach, and here I just want to supplement his point in two ways. First, it seems useful to further situate his position on the conventional landscape of American civil rights history, theory, and doctrine. Second, I suggest that certain of the more abstract and formal aspects of antidiscrimination law, which might be thought targets of Post's critique, actually are consistent with a contextualist approach, once we take account of law's own political context and its specificity as a set of social practices that incorporate ideals of legality, with their associated temptations of legalism.

Classical liberalism is suspicious of status hierarchies. Indeed, the equality aspect of the liberal ideal of a society of free and equal individuals seems originally to have meant simply that law should not define or maintain any castelike arrangements. Thus, nineteenth-century lib-

5. *See* pp. 23–39.
6. 443 U.S. 193, 208–09 (1979).

erals sought the abolition of slavery and supported the rights of non-Christians, nonwhites, women, servants, paupers, and immigrants to own property, make contracts, engage in lawful occupations, travel, and change residences on equal legal terms with members of the most favored class. The idea was that every competent adult should fit within a single legal category, that of "free person," or simply "person." The Roman and medieval "law of persons," with its complex status hierarchies, was to wither away.

Modern antidiscrimination law is in a sense a natural extension of that classical liberal ideal of equality under law. Slavery was to be abolished, not just the law of slavery repealed. The removal of formal legal status hierarchies left behind entrenched social norms that often effectively denied equal opportunity in much the same way as the old legal restraints. Customary norms still, for example, kept qualified blacks and women from holding many jobs, using some public accommodations, and owning or renting real property.

At the same time, the rise of the modern administrative state put in place the kind of legal machinery that could be directed against such nominally private structures of power. In the age of the regulatory state, it came to be seen as an additional requirement of the liberal ideal of legal equality that government should combat discriminatory social practices that served to maintain the functional effects of the old legal restrictions.

The first step, the abolition of formal legal status hierarchies, could be undertaken without choosing a theoretical framework for the liberal civil rights project. A sociological/contextual argument might well have been made for the classical liberal conclusion that every competent adult should have the single legal status of person, and we see at least the suggestion of such arguments in the work of historically and sociologically inclined writers like Maine and Durkheim. But the conclusion followed equally well from a more abstract and philosophical justification along Kantian lines—the principle that justice always and everywhere requires blindness to the particularities by which we separate individuals into social and cultural groups. The law of status could then be conceived as reduced to a single principle: Each free rational actor (legal translation: each competent adult) has, by virtue of that fact alone, the legal status of free person. The sole concern of the law is with what you do, not who you are, and this principle is to be understood abstractly and universally.

However, the second or modern step—the attack on social as distinguished from formal legal status hierarchies—requires a choice between an abstract and a contextual account. First, modern antidiscrimination law requires identifying those social practices that operate as functional equivalents of the old formal restrictions. There is no simple formal test that can do this; many social practices work to the practical disadvantage of identifiable social groups, but they do so legitimately. We do not believe that equality of opportunity guarantees equality of result. We have to distinguish invidiously discriminatory practices from neutral and legitimate social sorting mechanisms, and this requires a good deal of sociological knowledge, whether systematic or intuitive. (Why were the racially segregated bathrooms of Jim Crow so clearly invidious, whereas bathrooms segregated by sex equally clearly are not?)

Further, modern civil rights law requires deliberate strategic intervention into social life. The aim is to approximate the distribution of benefits and burdens that would have obtained had the old formal restraints not been carried forward through their surrogate discriminatory customs and social norms. Social engineering like this requires understanding how norm structures work and how law can effectively counter their caste-preserving effects. By contrast, the first or formal stage of civil rights law required nothing more than the identification and repeal of laws that openly imposed unequal status hierarchies.

One solution is simply to deny that the social intricacies exist, or at least refuse to deal with them through law. Some contemporary classical liberals would just carry forward the assumptions (e.g., the true inner self; you can't tell a book by its cover) that worked well in implementing the first stage of the law of equal opportunity. But as Post shows, these assumptions run into trouble when applied within modern antidiscrimination law.

When the rhetorical distinction between books and covers gets translated into legal doctrine, it naturally emerges as a distinction between biology and culture. Socially constructed race and gender differences are superficial, and hence to be disregarded in the law's allocation of burdens and benefits. Only biologically based differences are real, hence only proven biological necessity justifies differential treatment of the members of the former status groups. Because there are few if any provable and legally relevant biological differences between the races, we should strictly scrutinize all racially differential practices. By contrast, although many gender-based distinctions are socially constructed and must be abolished, some are justified by genuine biological differences — hence, intermediate scrutiny and the bona fide occupational qualification exception in gender discrimination law.

But as Post shows, these explanations will not hold up when they are examined in detail. Particularly in the area of gender discrimination, judges cannot sensibly and honestly decide cases without making distinctions that have little or nothing to do with the line between social construction and biological necessity. Thus the law allows men to be rejected as nursing home attendants for female patients,[7] but requires that women be allowed to guard male prisoners.[8] This is so even though gendered privacy conventions involving nudity in the presence of the opposite sex are the difficulty in both cases. A Playboy Club can require its waiters to be female, but airlines cannot require the same of flight attendants, even though the same "sex appeal for male customers" business rationale underlies both policies.[9] Employers can require that men, but not women, have short hair and wear ties, and they can require women, but not men, to wear skirts[10] — although the justification for the differential treatment is not biology but gendered hair and dress conventions. Even in the area of race, few believe that casting actors in roles to match for race is the kind of injustice that employment discrimination laws were meant to prohibit — though, again, the practice is rooted not in biology but in historically rooted cultural conventions governing theatrical portrayal.

In general, the creation and enforcement of modern antidiscrimination law involves the attempt to identify for elimination forms of dif-

7. *See* Post, pp. 33–34.
8. *See* p. 35.
9. *See* pp. 30–31.
10. *See* pp. 31–32, 36–39.

ferential treatment that are, to invoke a conclusory but still useful doctrinal term, invidious. In the examples noted above, gender (or race) differentiations are acceptable when they are based on conventions that are regarded as neutral — not part of the racial or gender caste system.

The contextual approach, if accepted, would influence legislators, judges, and commentators to confront openly the difficulties of drawing lines between invidious and innocent differentiation. By contrast, the abstracted approach, with its rhetorical attachment to treating all socially constructed differentiation as suspect, hides these questions — while still requiring that we answer them. This point should persuade even those who do not agree with each distinction drawn by the courts in Post's examples, as long as they are viewed as the kinds of distinctions that judges must make to decide discrimination cases sensibly. No such distinctions could be made if, as the official rhetoric suggests, civil rights law were really committed to requiring blindness to all gender or race distinctions derived from convention or practice rather than based on biological difference.

I think my amplification of the contextual approach, which draws attention to the two stages of civil rights law — the classical and the modern — can offer some help in explaining, for example, the differences to which Post points between the law of gender and race discrimination. Recall that the abstract approach can justify differential treatment only on the basis of biological necessity and must say (however inconsistently with the actual course of decisions) that it condemns all conventional or socially constructed grounds for differentiation.

The social-biological distinction cannot explain the law's quite different treatment of racial and sexual separate-but-equal segregation. It is a truism of civil rights law that mandated racial segregation, even with materially equal facilities, is invidiously discriminatory. By contrast, sex segregation has been readily accepted with respect to bathroom, dressing, and sleeping facilities and found debatable on a case-by-case basis with respect to separate educational facilities for males and females.

We cannot plausibly explain these differences in treatment on the ground that biological differences justify the sex but not the race segregation. They make much more sense when one considers contemporary civil rights law as a strategic response to the social norms left in the wake of dismantled status hierarchies that valued whites over blacks, and men over women.

A strategic response must take account of the nature of the enemy, and the different histories of racism and patriarchy help explain the varied responses to "separate-but-equal" segregation. Racism and its legal manifestations have always rested squarely on an ideology of white supremacy. Attempts to justify segregation as a path to the separate development of different but equally valuable human groups have never been more than transparent rationalizations devised by white supremacists in response to external restraints on the simpler forms of discrimination.

By contrast, the evolution of the ideology governing relations between the sexes has been more complex. From an earlier normative order based on the conception of women as clearly inferior, placed below men on the Great Chain of Being, the nineteenth century developed an ideology of separate spheres—that men and women were of equal worth, though different in their natures. Men were stronger, more logical, and more decisive, and thus more fit for the public spheres of marketplace, forum, and battlefield. Women were more flexible, intuitive, nurturing, and pure, and thus more suited for the private realms of home, church, and salon.

Simple rationalization of male domination played a major role in this ideology, but there was more to it than that. The separate spheres theory was, in certain respects, a genuine first step on the road to legal and social equality for women. Indeed, the notion that women are importantly different from men but equal to them in worth still survives in the influential "difference" strand of contemporary feminist theory. The ambiguous legacy of separate spheres ideology means that contemporary sex discrimination law must make a nuanced distinction between the manifestations of that ideology that are simply ruses for male supremacy and those that are reflections of egalitarianism.

This brief discussion of separate-but-equal segregation is meant to suggest how conceptual division of civil rights law into its two stages —classical and modern—might be helpful in making the contextual judgments that Post's approach requires. It works most clearly in the cases of race and sex discrimination, but modern law also prohibits discrimination on other grounds—age, disability, and sexual orientation, among others. How can it apply to these?

Recall that race and sex discrimination were embodied in well-defined and legally sanctioned social hierarchies, which liberal reformers began to attack long ago. That assault on the legally entrenched caste system was the "first stage" I have referred to in my account. But no similar first stage can be identified with respect to contemporary laws prohibiting discrimination on the basis of age, sexual orientation, and disability, which are not generally enacted in response to a history of legally formalized status hierarchy. Still, the two-stage analysis can, with appropriate modification, be of some guidance in formulating a contextual version of these bodies of law.

The basic idea of the contextual approach is to identify and articulate the terms of the hierarchy that the civil rights laws in question seek to dismantle. Sometimes, as with race and gender, these hierarchies will have been given formal legal definition. In other cases, as with age and the like, the present structure of discriminatory social norms may lack clear legal antecedents in a defined status system.

In these latter cases, contemporary lawmakers cannot identify invidious discrimination by looking for those aspects of a social hierarchy that mirror a past legal status regime. They must ascertain the content of the social hierarchy directly, through either systematic or (by default) impressionistic ethnography. In the latter case, they are like native speakers feeling their way to the grammatical patterns that structure their own language without the help of scientific linguists. Having found "the enemy"—that fragment of a social practice that sufficiently resembles an invidious legal status hierarchy of the kind classical liberalism condemned—the lawmakers must then formulate a strategy to dismantle this structure, or at least remedy its unjust effects, within the limitations set by legal institutions and practices.

Of course the same mix of intuitive and systematic ethnography supplements the formal use of legal history in the development of modern race and gender law. The difference is that in the case of age, disability, and sexual orientation, the guidance from formal legal history is absent or less helpful.

Does a sociological account like Post's simply mean that antidiscrimination law must proceed case by case, identifying and attempting to reform group-based practices that are found, taking all factors into account, to be unacceptably invidious? It might seem so at first glance, but a second look at the implications of a contextual approach should correct any first impression that sociological jurisprudence is inevitably so informal or undisciplined.

Post's approach does suggest a flexible and situational set of responses to the various categories of discrimination. The process of identifying invidious social practices depends on (often intuitive) sociological insight; designing a legal campaign to eradicate those norms calls for strategic acumen. There are no handbooks or recipes that make either of these tasks routine or mechanical, and it can be expected that quite variable judgments will be reached about what practices are unacceptably invidious, and what remedies are appropriate and effective in dealing with them.

Indeed in his specific examples, Post does call for judges in discrimination cases to make subtler distinctions than the rhetoric of the dominant abstract approach encourages. He suggests that a judge distinguishing the nursing home attendant case[11] from the prison guard case[12] is considering the differing weights conventionally attributed to the privacy interests of elderly female patients and male prison inmates and should make any such consideration explicit.[13]

But this example should make us notice a set of factors that will work to limit the degree of flexibility and nuance we might otherwise expect to find in a contextualized body of antidiscrimination law. As Post emphasizes, civil rights law is the effort to reform a unique set of cultural and historic practices, those structuring castelike social hierarchies. As he mentions, but does not emphasize, the effort to reform

11. *See* pp. 33–34.
12. *See* p. 35.
13. *See id.*

those customs is channeled through another set of social practices — our legal institutions. Within those legal practices is a complex of traditions that constitute the political ideal we call "the rule of law," the notion that coercive state power should be limited so that we may have a government of laws.

It should be noted that when the set of traditions constituting the rule of law create barriers to our most worthy strivings for social change, we are likely to condemn them as "legalism." Legalism and the rule of law are not easily separated from each other, perhaps because they are two sides of the same coin. But a constitutive element of our legal institutions is the aspiration that law should be relatively objective and neutral, in the sense that it can be administered to roughly the same effect by individuals with different views on the partisan conflicts of the day.

Now let's return to the contrast between the prison, which can't exclude women from guarding male prisoners, and the nursing home, which need not hire male attendants for female patients. One aspect of the rule of law — indeed, an aspect deeply implicated in civil rights law itself — is a preference for weighing the interests of individuals separately from their transitory legal status. Though it need not be decisive, this norm cuts against the practical and contextual tendency Post invokes in his explanation of the distinction made between the two cases. Our social mores do treat prisoners' expectations of privacy as less compelling than those of elderly female nursing home patients. But when we "think like lawyers," we identify this as a status-based distinction and as such to be resisted. A judge would be more likely than a politician or a social worker to reject the offered distinction, precisely because of the judge's acculturation in the ways of thinking that are distinctive to legal training and legal institutions.

If you think this effect of the judge's legal training is a salutary check in this case, you will speak reverently of the rule of law and its value in promoting equality. But if instead you think it is a rigid refusal to make a commonsense distinction, you will speak ruefully of the legalistic tendency to ignore real differences. Justice is blind, sometimes for good, sometimes for ill. In either case, the point remains that the law, even when understood as a set of socially embedded practices and not an abstract structure of norms and concepts, is an instrument that re-interprets and often redirects the force of the social impulses that drive its content and usually in a relatively formal direction.

More generally, we can say that ideals of legality would operate to restrain the tendency of the sociological approach to produce a highly situational law of discrimination. The rule of law and his evil twin, legalism, are alike in preferring objective rules to flexible standards. Thus, many of the doctrines that Post criticizes as historically crude and sociologically insensitive can nonetheless be defended as more imper-sonal and detached than the doctrinal alternatives that an unadulter-ated contextual approach would otherwise suggest.

Commentators inculcated in the legalist(ic) tradition will regard an unduly situational body of civil rights law not as a properly lawful structure of neutral rules and principles but as a reform project that im-poses an unacceptably managerial task on judges. Egalitarian lawyers will worry that if judges (who tend to be creatures of the establishment) are left alone to decide civil rights cases on the basis of particularized judgments of invidiousness, they will be too inclined to find familiar practices lawful. Conservative lawyers will worry that if liberal judges follow their ethnographic intuitions and strategic instincts, they will tend to find invidiousness everywhere and then impose a draconian regime of political correctness to stamp it out. Judges themselves, faced with decisions that engage burning social passions on both sides, will look for solutions that do not force them to take sides in too obviously political a way.

A practical response to these interacting concerns might well be a compromise on a relatively (though not absolutely) formal version of civil rights law. All parties, legalist and judicial, liberal and conserva-tive, fear the consequences of too much judicial discretion. All might then converge on the substitution of rules that, although relatively crude, are also relatively objective and thus stable, for the sociologi-cally nuanced and flexibly strategic responses that one would expect if Post's contextual approach were generally accepted. In practice, of course, any workable body of rules will leave considerable room for the exercise of situational judgment. But when we take account of the addi-tional context supplied by politics, and by the acculturation of lawyers and judges in a legalist tradition, we may reintroduce a considerable amount of the formalism we were originally inclined to displace.

The resulting law of civil rights might look something like the law we have today. Yet such a body of law would not rest to any degree on any lawyer's or judge's failure to understand the cultural and historical specificity of the social norms through which we construct race, gender, and so on. Its formalistic and legalistic features would be grounded not in philosophical error but in the practices and practicalities, themselves quite culturally and historically specific, that make up the institutions and environment of a particular legal system at a particular time.

My point is not that a sociologically grounded critique of the kind represented by this remarkable essay devours itself, and so is futile and should be avoided. Rather, I agree with the thrust of Post's argument and have tried to amplify it in what I hope is a helpful way. I do not believe that making the critique, and then qualifying it by reference to our legal culture's devotion to the rule of law (and hence its embroilment in legalism), simply leaves things where they were.

Emphasis on the fact that the rule-of-law/legalism complex is part of the context of law, and so of antidiscrimination law, does not take away the force of the contextualist critique. No doubt, in discussing issues of discrimination and prejudice, we will continue to recite to each other the maxim that you can't tell a book by its cover. But we should not confuse this sometimes useful nostrum with an inflexible axiom or a philosophical principle. We make a lot of judgments about what to read on the basis of what we know about books from their covers alone, and we could scarcely do otherwise.

In the same vein, the notion that the controversy over affirmative action can be resolved by simple application of a slogan about color blindness cannot survive Post's critique. Not only is there an important distinction between an abstract and a contextual approach to antidiscrimination law, but the contextual approach is better.

Reva B. Siegel | Discrimination in the

Eyes of the Law: How "Color Blindness" Discourse

Disrupts and Rationalizes Social Stratification

I am quite pleased to have this opportunity to comment on Robert Post's provocative essay "Prejudicial Appearances."[1] Post's effort to distinguish the "dominant conception" of antidiscrimination law from what he presents as a "sociological" account of the field intersects in striking ways with my own efforts to analyze status relations and their disestablishment from a sociohistorical vantage point. In this response, I would like to identify some key points of similarity and difference in our accounts, with a view to furthering consideration of what we might learn from a sociological approach to the field.

I have learned more than I can express from working with Robert Post over the years, yet I still find myself startled at the ways our intuitions about things of this world diverge and converge. In the long tradition of our long arguments, this response begins by emphasizing an important difference in our approaches to the question explored in his lecture, and winds up identifying a deep ground of methodological agreement between us.

1. Robert Post, "Prejudicial Appearances: The Logic of American Antidiscrimination Law," reproduced in this volume, pp. 1–53.

As I explore in the first part of this response, my own efforts to model antidiscrimination law from a dynamic, or sociohistorical, vantage point take as central to the field the problem of social stratification, a concept missing from Post's sociological account. In the remainder of this response, I argue that one needs a concept of social stratification — of status inequality among groups arising out of the interaction of social structure and social meaning — to make sense of the blindness trope at the heart of antidiscrimination law.

Parts II and III of this response offer such an account. Part II demonstrates how color blindness discourse functions as a semantic code and then illustrates how this semantic code can be used to characterize practices in ways that may either disrupt or rationalize social stratification. Part III of this response continues this sociohistorical analysis of color blindness discourse, examining how color blindness discourse works to disrupt or rationalize social stratification over time and under changing sociohistorical conditions.

So considered, sociohistorical analysis enables us to say considerably more about the purposes of equality law than Post has. Throughout his essay, Post suggests that a sociological understanding of antidiscrimination law would have us reshape race and gender conventions so as to promote the purposes of the law. But he never gives any hint as to what those purposes might be. Where Post remains agnostic in the debate over whether equality law is best served by an "antidiscrimination" or an "antisubordination" principle, I draw on sociohistorical analysis to show that a commitment to alleviating stratification has been central to the project of antidiscrimination law since the beginning of the Second Reconstruction. Yet, as I show, the same mode of analysis that demonstrates that antidiscrimination law has always endeavored to alleviate stratification also demonstrates the limitations of abstract principles (such as antidiscrimination or antisubordination) in guiding our critical practices.

In the final analysis, I concur with Post's view — so compellingly argued in his First Amendment scholarship — that a meta-principle abstracted from social practice cannot help us resolve many of the most pressing and controverted questions in law. At its best, a sociological, or sociohistorical, account of the problems addressed by antidiscrimination law reveals to us the nest of more particularized positive and normative questions to which tropes of blindness often blind us. At the end of the day, we must forge answers to these questions in history: as we argue over the justice of particular social relations, particular social practices, and particular social meanings, and as such conflicts produce changes in the very relations, practices, and meanings that sustain status inequality over time.

Sociological Approaches to Discrimination

This response opens with a brief sketch of Post's essay that cannot possibly do its full argument justice but does, I hope, identify the basic analytical framework that Post has identified as a "sociological" account of antidiscrimination law. I then draw on my own prior work to sketch, in similarly brief terms, a sociohistorical account of antidiscrimination law that diverges from Post's in one especially crucial dimension. On my account, the concept of social stratification is key to understanding antidiscrimination law and color blindness discourse, as I then undertake to demonstrate in the remaining parts of this response.

Post's Account of Antidiscrimination Law

In "Prejudicial Appearances," Post offers an account of the "dominant conception" of antidiscrimination law derived from the case law itself. Antidiscrimination law, he observes, "seeks to neutralize widespread forms of prejudice that pervasively disadvantage persons based on inaccurate judgments about their worth or capacities"[2] by "eliminating or carefully scrutinizing the use of stigmatizing characteristics as a ground for judgment."[3] As the Supreme Court explains: "In passing Title VII, Congress made the simple but momentous announcement that sex, race, religion, and national origin are not relevant to the selection, evaluation, or compensation of employees."[4]

Antidiscrimination law thus requires employers "to make decisions as if their employees did not exhibit forbidden characteristics, as if,

2. *See* p. 10.
3. *See* p. 12.
4. *Price Waterhouse v. Hopkins*, 490 U.S. 228, 239 (1989) (Brennan, J., plurality opinion).

for example, employees had no race or sex."[5] "This," Post observes, "is what underwrites the important trope of 'blindness.' . . . Blindness renders forbidden characteristics invisible; it requires employers to base their judgments instead upon the deeper and more fundamental grounds of 'individual merit' or 'intrinsic worth.' "[6] The law would have employers judge employees on the basis of what it deems to be relevant, rational, and legitimate criteria—the employee's ability to perform the job. As the Court observed in *Griggs*, "Congress has not commanded that the less qualified be preferred over the better qualified simply because of minority origins. Far from disparaging job qualifications as such, Congress has made such qualifications the controlling factor, so that race, religion, nationality, and sex become irrelevant."[7]

In passing, Post questions whether law ought to encourage employers to apprehend their employees in such purely instrumental terms,[8] but his challenge to the field is more fundamental. In "Prejudicial Appearances," Post contends that antidiscrimination law does not and cannot cause employers to make judgments about qualifications in a manner that is completely race and sex blind: "Law is made by the very persons who participate in the social practices that constitute race, gender, and beauty. It would be astonishing, therefore, if American antidiscrimination law could transcend these categories, if it could operate in a way that rendered them truly irrelevant."[9]

On Post's "sociological" account of the field, antidiscrimination law instead "alter[s] the norms by which sex is given social meaning."[10] Enforcement of the employment discrimination statute does not eliminate " 'the entire spectrum of disparate treatment of men and women resulting from sex stereotypes,' "[11] at least if "stereotypes" are understood as Post defines them—"the conventions that underwrite the so-

5. *See* p. 14.
6. *See id.*
7. *Griggs v. Duke Power Co.*, 401 U.S. 424, 436 (1971).
8. *See* pp. 16–18.
9. *See* p. 22.
10. *See* p. 26.
11. *County of Washington v. Gunther*, 452 U.S. 161, 180 (1981) (quoting *Los Angeles Dep't of Water & Power v. Manhart*, 435 U.S. 702, 707, n.13 [1978]) (emphasis removed).

cial practice of gender."[12] Instead, as Post illustrates through an analysis of the cases enforcing Title VII's prohibition against discrimination on the basis of sex,[13] Title VII interacts with "gender practices . . . in a selective manner."[14] The case law interpreting Title VII bars many gender-specific employment practices, but it authorizes others—notoriously, the enforcement of gender-specific dress and grooming codes[15] and gender-specific job assignments intended to protect customer privacy interests.[16] In short, enforcement of the federal employment discrimination statute may disrupt and transform existing gender norms, but it does not wholly obliterate them.

This, Post argues, is as it should be. On the sociological account, the law "does not ask whether 'stereotypic impressions' can be eliminated *tout court,* but rather how this alters and modifies such impressions."[17] Antidiscrimination law is a "social practice, which regulates other social practices"; courts should therefore strive to "reshape [race and gender] in ways that reflect the purposes of the law."[18]

Post goes on to offer reasons, apart from simple descriptive accuracy, for embracing this "sociological" account of antidiscrimination law over the "dominant conception" of the field.[19] But before assessing those reasons, I would like first to consider how Post's sociological account of the field both converges with and diverges from my own.

Supplementing the Sociological Account:
Stratification in Sociohistorical Perspective
For some years now, I have used legal-historical methods to explore problems in antidiscrimination law. When I first turned to history, it was to explore changes in race and gender relations during periods when conversation about social status was far more explicit than it is

12. *See* p. 23.
13. *See* pp. 23–39.
14. *See* p. 34.
15. *See* pp. 31–32, 36–38.
16. *See* pp. 33–34.
17. *See* p. 40.
18. *See* p. 22.
19. *See* pp. 39–52.

today. But, as I began to examine the changing structure of gender and race relations in late-nineteenth-century America, it occurred to me that I was examining a historical moment that is in important respects not unlike our own. In the aftermath of the Civil War, the nation began to experiment with disestablishing race and gender inequality. Law reform in this era sought to make whites and blacks more equal before the law and, in more halting ways, to affirm notions of sex equality, particularly in marriage. By looking at how the legal system began to disestablish gender and race inequality in the nineteenth century, we can learn something about the operations of antidiscrimination law today.

With questions of this sort in view, I have explored changes in the regulation of reproduction, violence, work, suffrage, and citizenship in the period after the Civil War.[20] For the purposes of this response, I will draw from my work several observations about the nature of race and sex discrimination, sociohistorically considered. This exercise will reveal deep grounds of agreement with the sociological account Post

---

20. *See, e.g.*, Reva B. Siegel, "Abortion as a Sex Equality Right: Its Basis in Feminist Theory," in *Mothers in Law: Feminist Theory and the Legal Regulation of Motherhood* 43 (Martha Albertson Fineman and Isabel Karpin eds., 1995) [hereinafter Siegel, "Abortion as Equality Right"]; Reva B. Siegel, "Collective Memory and the Nineteenth Amendment: Reasoning About 'the Woman Question' in the Discourse of Sex Discrimination," in *History, Memory, and the Law* 131 (Austin Sarat ed., 1999) [hereinafter Siegel, "Collective Memory"]; Reva B. Siegel, "Home as Work: The First Woman's Rights Claims Concerning Wives' Household Labor, 1850–1880," 103 *Yale L. J.* 1073 (1994) [hereinafter Siegel, "Home as Work"]; Reva B. Siegel, "Reasoning from the Body: An Historical Perspective on Abortion Regulation and Questions of Equal Protection," 44 *Stan. L. Rev.* 261 (1992) [hereinafter Siegel, "Reasoning from the Body"]; Reva B. Siegel, "The Modernization of Marital Status Law: Adjudicating Wives' Rights to Earnings, 1860–1930," 82 *Geo. L. J.* 2127 (1994) [hereinafter Siegel, "Modernization"]; Reva B. Siegel, "The Racial Rhetorics of Colorblind Constitutionalism: The Case of *Hopwood v. Texas*," in *Race and Representation: Affirmative Action* 29 (Robert Post and Michael Rogin eds., 1998) [hereinafter Siegel, "Colorblind Constitutionalism"]; Reva B. Siegel, " 'The Rule of Love': Wife Beating as Prerogative and Privacy," 105 *Yale L. J.* 2117 (1996) [hereinafter Siegel, "Rule of Love"]; Reva B. Siegel, "Valuing Housework: Nineteenth-Century Anxieties about the Commodification of Domestic Labor," 41 *Am. Behav. Sci.* 1437 (1998); Reva B. Siegel, "Why Equal Protection No Longer Protects: The Evolving Forms of Status-Enforcing State Action," 49 *Stan L. Rev.* 1111 (1997) [hereinafter Siegel, "Equal Protection"].

offers in "Prejudicial Appearances," but it will also expose some important grounds of difference.

Post describes antidiscrimination law as a social practice that regulates the social practices of race and gender, altering the conventions
that give such practices meaning.[21] While this is a helpful account, it
fails to describe certain fundamental features of the undertaking.

Considered concretely, antidiscrimination law regulates the social
practices that sustain the relative social position of whites and blacks,
men and women. A bit more abstractly, we might say that antidiscrimination law regulates the social practices that sustain group inequality. The group inequalities that concern antidiscrimination law are
typically those that are socially pervasive (articulated across social domains) and socially persistent (articulated over time). When inequality
among groups is structurally pervasive and persistent in this way, we
typically refer to it as a condition of *social stratification*.[22]

When we analyze race and gender inequality from a historical standpoint, we encounter relations of group inequality embedded in the social organization of work, reproduction, and sexuality as such activities
are structured in institutions such as slavery, the market, or marriage.
Indeed, from the standpoint of history, what is perhaps most visible is
the sheer heterogeneity of institutions, practices, stories, and reasons
that sustain the unequal social position of different groups over time.
Couched a bit more abstractly, we might say that social stratification
is constituted through features of (1) social structure (institutions or
practices) and (2) social meaning (stories or reasons). The elements of
social structure and social meaning that sustain stratification vary by
group and within groups, and they evolve over time as their legitimacy
is contested. In short, when considered from a historical standpoint,
discrimination has no transcontextual or fixed form.[23]

21. *See* pp. 21–39.

22. For an overview of some of the recent sociological literature on stratification, see
Social Stratification: Class, Race, and Gender in Sociological Perspective (David B. Grusky
ed., 1994).

23. *See, e.g.,* Siegel, "Equal Protection," *supra* note 20, at 1119; Siegel, "Modernization,"
supra note 20, at 2210–11; Siegel, "Rule of Love," *supra* note 20, at 2179. In other words,
I reject the legal-formalist assumption that, through abstract ("principled") reasoning,

A look at history discloses that the network of institutions, practices, and meanings that support social stratification varies by group, and within groups as well. There are a variety of institutions (e.g., market, family), practices (e.g., separation, role differentiation), and reasons (e.g., degradation, paternalism) employed to enforce the different social status of groups. And because persons are members of multiple status groups, there may well be considerable variation in the institutions, practices, and meanings that regulate the social position of different members of one group.[24]

Furthermore, the institutions, practices, and reasons that support group stratification vary over time as their legitimacy is contested. At any point in history, a society may view inequality in the distribution of social goods as lawful or illicit, just or unjust. Inequality in the distribution of material and dignitary goods among groups is periodically contested, and when the legitimacy of a particular distributive regime is successfully challenged, status-enforcing practices often evolve in rule structure and rationale, a dynamic I have called preservation-through-transformation.[25] Successful challenges to the legitimacy of a distribu-

---

we can adduce the kinds of social groups at which discrimination is directed or the kinds of social forms it assumes. Rather, these understandings emerge through social struggle, as various features of social stratification are contested over time. "Discrimination" and "prejudice" are names that we use to brand as illegitimate, practices and reasons that American society once viewed as perfectly legitimate.

24. *See, e.g.,* Siegel, "Abortion as Equality Right," *supra* note 20, at 58–59 (observing that the nineteenth-century campaign to criminalize abortion focused on birth-control practices of privileged women, and cautioning that it is important to ascertain the class and race salience of reproductive regulation, which can be "birth-compelling or birth-deterring in form"); Siegel, "Home as Work," *supra* note 20, at 1189–1205 (observing that during the Reconstruction era, when the woman's rights movement began to assert that wives' household labor inhibited them from attaining equality with their husbands, the movement's leadership advocated a reorganization of the family sphere in which women would perform household labor on a collective basis, with poor working women performing manual aspects of household labor for pay under the direction of "educated" women); Siegel, "Rule of Love," *supra* note 20, at 2134–41, 2150–70 (observing that during the Reconstruction era, the legal system punished at the whipping post poor and minority men accused of wife beating, while extending privacy-based immunities to more privileged men accused of similar conduct).

25. Siegel, "Rule of Love," *supra* note 20, at 2175–88.

tive regime redefine what counts as a fair or just practice or rationale for allocating social goods, and practices and reasons once thought reasonable are thus periodically recharacterized as wrongful.[26]

Since the Civil War, the American legal system has played an increasingly self-conscious role in regulating the distributive regimes that sustain group stratification. Of course, law works both to disestablish and to legitimate the distributive regimes that sustain group stratification. Consider, for example, the transition from slavery to segregation. As law confers formal equality on groups, it disturbs the institutions, practices, and meanings that maintain social stratification, and, to the extent it does so, incremental changes in the relative social position of groups may result.[27]

Analyzing Color Blindness through the Lens of Stratification

When the sociological account of antidiscrimination law that Post offers in "Prejudicial Appearances" is elaborated in these ways, we can say something more about how the practice of "blindness" works to transform and preserve relations of race and gender inequality. The concept of stratification or group inequality that is missing from Post's account plays a key role here. One needs a concept of social stratification, of status inequality among groups arising out of the interaction of social structure and social meaning, in order to make sense of the blindness trope at the heart of antidiscrimination law. For it is the social condition of racial stratification that makes the concept of colorblindness intelligible as a distributive principle.[28] When we say we are distributing goods and opportunities in a race- and gender-blind fashion, we recognize group identity but ignore the ordinary status consequences of

---

26. *See, e.g.,* Siegel, "Equal Protection," *supra* note 20, at 1146–48.

27. *See* generally *id.* (illustrating how, during both the First and Second Reconstruction, interpretation of the Equal Protection Clause disturbed and preserved the subordinate social position of African Americans); Siegel, "Colorblind Constitutionalism," *supra* note 20, at 48–57 (tracing discourse of racial privacy during the First and Second Reconstructions and illustrating how an understanding of racial equality at law in each era presupposed the perpetuation of racial inequality in social fact). For an account of changes in gender status law during this period, *see* Siegel, "Rule of Love," *supra* note 20.

28. Siegel, "Colorblind Constitutionalism," *supra* note 20, at 51.

group identity for purposes of the relevant social transaction.[29] Differently put, blindness tropes are concerned with counteracting the normal status-linked benefits and detriments of group membership.[30]

Even so, practices of group-blind distribution generally alleviate group stratification without eradicating it. How is this so? The blindness trope is, as I have argued, no less a legal fiction than the doctrine of marital unity or the concept of equality in the eyes of the law.[31] As I will now illustrate, instability and slippage in discourses of race and gender, as well as the idiom of discrimination itself, allow this society to embrace principles of group-blind distribution without disestablishing group stratification. In short, antidiscrimination law contains its own complex mode of representing race and gender and of representing their transcendence, and these representations play a crucial part in the social construction of race and gender.[32]

In the ensuing discussion I will first illustrate the important role that representational conventions play in debates over the legitimacy of distributive practices and then proceed to consider in more detail how the discourse of color blindness itself works to disrupt and to rationalize the practices that sustain group inequality.

Representational Conventions in Debates
about the Legitimacy of Distributive Practices
Debates over the practices that sustain group inequality generate their own representational conventions — representations of the social

29. *See id.*

30. *Cf.* Joseph Tussman and Jacobus tenBroek, "The Equal Protection of the Laws," 37 *Calif. L. Rev.* 339, 354 (1949) (proposing doctrines of "suspect classification" and "rigid scrutiny" whose "content, at any particular time, will depend upon the area in which the principle of equality is struggling against the recurring forms of claims to special and unequal status — whether along racial, religious, economic, or even political, lines").

31. *See* Reva B. Siegel, "In the Eyes of the Law: Reflections on the Authority of Legal Discourse," in *Law's Stories: Narrative and Rhetoric in the Law* 225, 227 (Peter Brooks and Paul Gewirtz eds., 1996).

32. *Cf.* Michael Omi and Howard Winant, *Racial Formation in the United States: From the 1960s to the 1990s* at 55–56 (2d ed. 1994) (advocating an approach to "racial formation" that understands race as growing out of interaction of "both social structure and cultural representation").

groups in question as well as of those aspects of social structure and social meaning that sustain the groups' relative social status. For example, even those with no formal training in law understand that "crack cocaine" is a "race-neutral" concept in the criminal justice system but race-identified in social practice. Similarly they understand that "domestic labor," "child care," "rape," and "single parent" are "gender-neutral" in law and gender-identified in social practice. Given the explosive questions about distribution that drive debates about the legitimacy of the practices that sustain group inequality, it is not terribly surprising that a society would develop specialized ways of arguing about the justice of its social practices and the modes of regulation to which they are properly subject. More striking is the way that linguistically competent actors—with and without formal training in law—manipulate these representational conventions in debates about the justice of distributive practices. Those engaged in argument continually exploit semantic instability in the positive and normative terms employed to characterize groups and practices, yet participants in the debate appear to be only intermittently cognizant of the degree to which this is so.

To start with a seemingly simple case, what does it mean when we say that a rule classifies "on the basis of" race or sex? We often talk as if the meaning of this claim were transparent and uncontroverted; in fact it is not. Sometimes the Supreme Court reasons that for a rule to classify on the basis of sex, the rule must apply only to group members; but sometimes the Court reasons that the rule must apply to all group members. For example, in equal protection doctrine, the Court uses this dodge to avoid characterizing policies concerning pregnant women as sex-based,[33] so that, in the eyes of the law, abortion policies are not.[34] Along similar lines, the "sex-plus" doctrine, which currently

---

33. See Geduldig v. Aiello, 417 U.S. 484, 496–97 n.20 (1974) ("The program divides potential recipients into two groups—pregnant women and nonpregnant persons. While the first group is exclusively female, the second includes members of both sexes.").

34. See, e.g., Bray v. Alexandria Women's Health Clinic, 506 U.S. 263, 271 (1993) ("'While it is true . . . that only women can become pregnant, it does not follow that every legislative classification concerning pregnancy is a sex-based classification'" Quoting Geduldig v. Aiello, 417 U.S. at 484, 496 n.20) (reaffirming Geduldig and applying its holding that

protects sex-specific grooming and dress codes, holds that policies that apply to some but not all group members do not classify on the basis of sex, unless they concern an immutable trait or a fundamental right.[35] On this account, employers may prohibit women from wearing pants or men from wearing dresses without discriminating on the basis of sex.[36] (Discrimination on the basis of sexual orientation can be expressed in sex-plus terms—as, for example, a refusal to hire men who desire men—but courts simply exclude homophobic hiring criteria from the ambit of sex-plus doctrine, on the grounds that courts should not extend Title VII to forms of discrimination that Congress did not intend to prohibit.)[37]

Yet as we examine the characterization of practices as distinct from rules, we discover that practices that pertain to some, but not all, group members are often characterized as discriminating "on the basis of sex." Consider, for example, sexual harassment doctrine. A man makes overtures to a woman. By reason of a heterosexual presumption, coupled with what Kenji Yoshino terms a monosexual presumption,[38] courts assume that a putative harasser will make such overtures only to women.[39]

---

classifications pertaining to pregnancy are not necessarily sex-based to abortion in the course of interpreting animus provision of civil rights statute).

35. See *Willingham v. Macon Tel. Publ'g Co.*, 507 F.2d 1084, 1091 (5th Cir. 1975).

36. See, e.g., *Lanigan v. Bartlett & Co. Grain*, 466 F. Supp. 1388, 1391 (W.D.Mo. 1979) (applying "sex-plus" doctrine to uphold discharge of female employee who violated dress code by wearing a pantsuit, reasoning that "plaintiff's affection for pantsuits is not an 'immutable characteristic'"); cf. *Devine v. Lonschein*, 621 F. Supp. 894, 897 (S.D.N.Y. 1985) ("At least until that dreadful day when unisex identity of dress and appearance arrives, judicial officers . . . are entitled to some latitude in differentiating between male and female attorneys, within the context of decorous professional behavior and appearance.").

37. See, e.g., *DeSantis v. Pacific Tel. & Tel. Co.*, 608 F.2d 327, 331 (9th Cir. 1979) ("We must again reject appellants' efforts to 'bootstrap' Title VII protection for homosexuals. . . . Whether dealing with men or women the employer is using the same criterion: it will not hire or promote a person who prefers sexual partners of the same sex. Thus this policy does not involve different decisional critera for the sexes.").

38. Courts assume that the harasser is either heterosexual or homosexual, but not bisexual. See Kenji Yoshino, "The Epistemic Contract of Bisexual Erasure," 52 *Stan. L. Rev.* 353 (2000).

39. See, e.g., *Oncale v. Sundowner Offshore Servs.*, 523 U.S. 75, 80 (1998) ("Courts and

Still it flies in the face of social understanding to say that he would make such overtures to all women. (Early on, sex-plus doctrine supplied a defense to claims of sexual harassment.)[40] Even if he did so, the law would not characterize such behavior as "discriminating" "on the basis of sex" unless the recipient, by her conduct, communicated that it was unwelcome.[41] Recent debates over harassment law merely drive to the surface the socially contingent act of characterization that occurs whenever we make judgments about practices that we claim discriminate on the basis of race or sex—a problem already familiar to us in debates over the concept of discriminatory intent.[42]

So when we say that an employer does not discriminate on the basis of race or sex, what exactly are we saying? As a doctrinal matter, it turns out that we are saying many different, and sometimes contradictory, things—and these terms are likely to have still other meanings to persons not familiar with some of the more arcane ways doctrine characterizes social practices. Yet color- and gender-blind discourse is more than indeterminate; it is partial. Race and gender stratification is sustained by many social practices and reasons, but antidiscrimination

---

juries have found the inference of discrimination easy to draw in most male-female sexual harassment situations, because the challenged conduct typically involves explicit or implicit proposals of sexual activity; it is reasonable to assume those proposals would not have been made to someone of the same sex.").

40. *See, e.g., Barnes v. Costle,* 561 F.2d 983, 990–91 & n.57 (D.C. Cir. 1977) (citing sex-plus cases and attempting to distinguish problem of sexual harassment).

41. *Meritor Savings Bank v. Vinson,* 477 U.S. 57, 68 (1986) ("The gravamen of any sexual harassment claim is that the alleged sexual advances were 'unwelcome.'" [quoting 29 CFR § 1604.11(a) (1985)]). Opponents of affirmative action, such as Justice Scalia, are the first to emphasize that gender-differentiating conduct is a necessary but not sufficient condition for liability in the sexual harassment context; the putatively harassing conduct must still be judged unwelcome, offensive, or pervasive before a court will declare that it discriminates on the basis of sex. *See Oncale,* 523 U.S. at 81 (holding that Title VII "does not reach genuine but innocuous differences in the ways men and women routinely interact with members of the same sex and of the opposite sex. The prohibition of harassment on the basis of sex requires neither asexuality nor androgyny in the workplace; it forbids only behavior so objectively offensive as to alter the 'conditions' of the victim's employment").

42. *See, e.g.,* Siegel, "Equal Protection," *supra* note 20, at 1141 n.57 (discussing the literature criticizing discriminatory purpose doctrine).

law constrains and delegitimates only some of them.[43] A society may thus embrace group-blind practices of distribution that alter without eradicating the social stratification of groups.

Color Blindness: Representing Race in Debates over Practices that Sustain Group Inequality

Once we begin to attend to the highly specialized ways in which anti-discrimination law represents race and discrimination, we can describe more precisely how color blindness discourse both constrains and legitimates practices that maintain racial stratification. To this end, I will first examine the distinctive ways in which tropes of race are employed in claims about color blindness and then consider how this rhetorical system is used to characterize the social practices that enforce and perpetuate the differential status of racial groups. This analysis will demonstrate how color blindness discourse works both to destabilize and to rationalize social stratification.

To illustrate the specialized and often contradictory ways that anti-discrimination law makes assertions about "race" as it evaluates the justice of our distributive practices, I will be working with some usage distinctions Neil Gotanda identifies in his influential article, "A Critique of 'Our Constitution Is Color-Blind.'"[44] Gotanda observes that the meaning of the term *race* varies significantly in Supreme Court cases and in ways that the Court does not generally acknowledge. Gotanda identifies four very different modes of talking about "race" in the antidiscrimination case law, which he calls "status-race," "formal-race," "historical-race," and "culture-race."[45] "Status-race" refers to the kinds of claims about race that the law might link to stereotypes, prejudice, or racism. "Formal-race" is the mode of talking about race that civil rights law has developed to oppose status-race claims; "formal-race" claims attempt to counteract status-race claims by practices of "racial nonrecognition" or color blindness premised on the view that race is

---

43. *See, e.g., supra* text accompanying notes 25–27, 33–37, and *infra* text accompanying notes 71–81.

44. Neil Gotanda, "A Critique of 'Our Constitution Is Color-Blind.'" 44 *Stan. L. Rev.* 1 (1991).

45. *Id.* at 3–4.

socially and morally irrelevant, a matter of appearance or skin color only. "Historical-race" is the way courts talk about race when describing differences in the social situation of racial groups or their individual members that are attributable to past or current discrimination. By contrast, "culture-race" approaches differences in the outlook and mores of racial groups or their individual members as more lasting features of group identity, treating race as a species of ethnicity, a concept at work when racial difference is celebrated as a form of diversity or otherwise judged by critics such as Dinesh D'Souza.[46]

Though the ensuing discussion will explore shifting legal usages of the term *race,* I note at the outset that one could extend Gotanda's analysis of the different forms of racial rhetoric to the case of gender, especially if one is looking for gender analogues to the concept of "formal-race" and the practice of color blindness or racial nonrecognition. For example, in ruling that gender-based peremptory strikes in jury selection are unconstitutional, Justice O'Connor observed: "We know that like race, gender matters. . . . [O]ne need not be a sexist to share the intuition that in certain cases a person's gender and resulting life experience will be relevant to his or her view of the case." [47] Yet she acknowledged that "today's decision severely limits a litigant's ability to act on this intuition, for the import of our holding is that any correlation between a juror's gender and attitudes is irrelevant as a matter of constitutional law." [48] Restrictions on the peremptory challenge, in matters of gender as in matters of race, amount to "a special rule of relevance, a statement about what this Nation stands for, rather than a statement of fact." [49] In this passage, O'Connor is unusually forthright in acknowledging multiple and specialized modes of talking about race

46. *See id.* at 4. For contrasting usage of the culture-race concept, compare *Regents of the University of California v. Bakke,* 438 U.S. 265, 316–19 (1978) (Powell, J., concurring) (reasoning that race may be used as a factor in educational admissions to enhance the diversity of the student body), with Siegel, "Colorblind Constitutionalism," *supra* note 20, at 52–55 (discussing commentators, such as Dinesh D'Souza, who argue that racial hierarchy reflects the cultural "merits" of different racial groups).
47. *J.E.B. v. Alabama,* 511 U.S. 127, 148–49 (1994) (O'Connor, J., concurring).
48. *Id.* at 149.
49. *Id.* (quoting *Brown v. North Carolina,* 479 U.S. 940, 941–42 [1986]).

and gender in the case law. Most commonly, antidiscrimination discourse slides — sometimes unconsciously, sometimes adventitiously — from formal to historical or cultural discourses about race and gender, and back again.[50]

It is by observing how these different modes of race talk interact in doctrinal claims about race discrimination that we can begin to understand how color blindness discourse functions as a semantic code. But to crack the code, we first need to consider more carefully how each of these modes of race talk supports or undermines claims about the instrumental rationality of regulatory decisions, claims that — as Robert Post has observed — now dominate color blindness talk.[51] Questions concerning the instrumental rationality of regulatory decisions have come to dominate color blindness discourse as it has been doctrinally elaborated in the Second Reconstruction because of the particular legal-process rationale through which antidiscrimination law has justified judicial review of such decisions.[52] When antidiscrimination law

50. See, e.g., Gotanda, supra note 44, at 36–52 (observing the movement between "formal" and "historical" usages of race in debates concerning race-conscious measures such as affirmative action); Siegel, "Colorblind Constitutionalism," supra note 20, at 41–47 (illustrating how the decision in Hopwood v. Texas, 78 F.3d 932 [5th Cir. 1996], employs contradictory uses of race in the course of analyzing diversity and remedial justifications for affirmative action).

51. See pp. 17–19.

52. See Bruce A. Ackerman, "Beyond Carolene Products," 98 Harv. L. Rev. 713, 713–15 (1985) ("The Carolene solution is to seize the high ground of democratic theory and establish that the challenged legislation was produced by a highly defective process.") (observing that the current rationale for judicial protection of minority rights was developed at a time when the Supreme Court was repudiating constitutional doctrines restricting New Deal legislation and was therefore preoccupied with the countermajoritarian difficulty). To appreciate how this legal-process narrative translates questions of discrimination into problems of instrumental rationality, see, for example, Gerald Gunther, "The Supreme Court, 1971 Term — Foreword: In Search of Evolving Doctrine on a Changing Court: A Model for a Newer Equal Protection," 86 Harv. L. Rev. 1, 20–21 (1972) ("Modest interventionism would certainly differ from the 'all-out tolerance' of the old equal protection and from the attitude of the hands off due process era. It would place a greater burden on the state to come forth with explanations about the contributions of its means to its ends. But that demand would reinforce, not conflict with . . . the Court's modern role [in] safeguarding the structure of the political process. . . . Means scrutiny . . . can improve the quality of the political process — without second-guessing

asks whether discrimination has occurred, it typically inquires whether the challenged action differentiates among persons "rationally," examining how persons are grouped or classified with respect to "traits" that might be "relevant" to the "purpose" of the regulatory action or law.[53] For this reason, I would now like to examine in somewhat more detail the different forms of race talk Gotanda has identified and then to consider how antidiscrimination law moves among these usages as it makes claims about the instrumental rationality and distributive justice of regulatory decisions.

Gotanda calls the mode of speaking about race associated with white supremacy or racial prejudice status-race.[54] Status-race claims are the conventional ascriptive claims about race that justify a status regime. We might note some additional characteristics of status-race claims. Status-race claims are often group-categorical; that is, they often attribute traits exclusively to members of one racial group or another. In their most conventional form, status-race claims differentiate superordinate and subordinate groups by attributing to members of each

---

the substantive validity of its results."). For accounts that situate the preoccupations of the legal process school in the larger intellectual movements of the post–World War II era, *see* Morton J. Horwitz, *The Transformation of American Law, 1870–1960: The Crisis of Legal Orthodoxy* 250–68 (1992); Edward A. Purcell, *The Crisis of Democratic Theory: Scientific Naturalism and the Problem of Value* (1973); Gary Peller, "Neutral Principles in the 1950s," 21 *U. Mich. J. L. Reform* 561 (1988); *cf.* Post, *supra* note 1, pp. 15–16 and n.68 (tracing the blindness trope in antidiscrimination law to a Rawlsian conception of justice; further noting that Rawls interprets the concept of rationality appropriate to the original position in economic terms, as a question concerning "the most effective means to given ends").

53. For the foundational statement of this approach, *see* Tussman and tenBroek, *supra* note 30, at 347 (presenting discrimination as a problem concerning the instrumental rationality of classifications, and offering a now-famous series of diagrams that "make it possible to assess the rationality of regulatory means given a stipulated regulatory purpose"). For an overview of some of the key cases and law review articles that translated this "legal-process" approach to discrimination into the strict-scrutiny framework that still governs the review of claims of race discrimination, see Paul Brest and Sanford Levinson, *Processes of Constitutional Decisionmaking: Cases and Materials* 554–79 (3d ed. 1992) (excerpting, *inter alia*, articles by Tussman and tenBroek, John Ely, and Gerald Gunther).

54. Gotanda, *supra* note 44, at 37.

group opposing traits that help explain their relative social status.[55] Thus, a familiar status-race claim is that whites are hardworking and blacks are lazy.[56] Status-race claims assume that race is a simple and sensible basis for explaining and organizing social relationships.

Formal-race talk arises as part of this society's effort to delegitimate status-race claims,[57] and is the mode of talking about race that we associate with civil rights law and color blindness. A familiar assertion within formal-race discourse is: "It is wrong to discriminate on the basis of race because the mere fact of race or skin color has no moral or social relevance." Like status-race talk, formal-race talk reasons about race in group-categorical terms. Formal-race talk assumes that race is a biological or physiological trait that all individuals possess and by which they can be differentiated into groups.[58] Yet, unlike status-race talk and in direct opposition to it, formal-race talk insists that race is a trait that has no social relevance.[59] On this view, it is irrational to distinguish persons by race.

A society intent on repudiating conventional status-based understandings of race does have other modes of talking about race. The modes of speech Gotanda identifies as "historical-race" and "culture-

55. For a detailed account of a status regime as an interlocking series of social meanings, *see* especially J. M. Balkin, "The Constitution of Status," 106 *Yale L. J.* 2313, 2321–35 (1997).

56. *Cf.* Kimberle Williams Crenshaw, "Race, Reform and Retrenchment: Transformation and Legitimation in Antidiscrimination Law," 101 *Harv. L. Rev.* 1331, 1370–74 (1988) (identifying a series of binary oppositions that help constitute the social meaning of white and black); *see also* J. M. Balkin, *Cultural Software: A Theory of Ideology* 216–18, 230–34 (1998) (discussing binary coding and nested oppositions that constitute race and gender). Not all status-race talk functions to differentiate members of superordinate and subordinate groups. Some status-race talk distinguishes among members of the subordinate group, identifying types who together constitute the group and so explain its subordinate social status. Status-race talk of this variety applies exclusively to group members, although to some but not all group members (for example, "the Uncle Tom" or "the uppity nigger").

57. *Cf. supra* text accompanying notes 28–29.

58. Paradoxically, color blindness discourse frequently asserts that the only real, although morally and socially irrelevant, aspect of race is appearance, "the mere color of one's skin."

59. *See* Gotanda, *supra* note 44, at 6 ("Formal-race implies that 'Black' and 'White' are mere racial classification labels, unconnected to social realities.").

race" are two of these. These modes of reasoning view race as a social formation, that is, as an aggregation of traits of potential social relevance. Historical-race understands the traits of racial groups as contingent, as arising out of a status system that is being dismantled over time. This mode of talking about race typically focuses on injuries sustained by members of subordinated groups.[60] By contrast, culture-race is that mode of talking that treats race as akin to ethnicity, as involving the distinctive forms of life that social groups work out over time.[61] In self-conscious opposition to status-race talk, historical-race claims and culture-race claims understand the traits that constitute race as group-salient and not group-categorical, as traits that are unevenly distributed in society and correlate closely, but by no means precisely, with racial group membership.

Now let us look more carefully at the special kinds of claims that color blindness or formal-race discourse makes about race, so that we can appreciate how color blindness claims interact with other modes of reasoning about race in arguments over the legitimacy of distributive practices. Color blindness or formal-race discourse is in fact a highly specialized form of race talk that shares some features in common with the status-race usages it was developed to combat. As we have seen, from the standpoint of formal-race discourse, race is a fixed yet radically empty feature of every person's identity. Like traditional biological conceptions of race, formal-race discourse views race as an empirically determinate feature of persons, but unlike traditional biological conceptions of race, formal-race discourse asserts that race has no socially relevant content. For example, in *Hopwood v. Texas*,[62] the Fifth Circuit quotes Richard Posner asserting this basic tenet of the color blindness creed: " 'The use of a racial characteristic to establish a presumption that the individual also possesses other, and socially rele-

---

60. *See id.* at 40 ("In historical-race usage, racial categories describe relations of oppression and unequal power. Historical-race usage of Black does not have the same meaning as usage of white: Black is the reification of subordination; white is the reification of privilege and superordination.").

61. *See id.* at 56 ("Culture-race includes all aspects of culture, community, and consciousness.").

62. 78 F.3d 932 (5th Cir. 1996).

vant, characteristics, exemplifies, encourages, and legitimizes the mode of thought and behavior that underlies most prejudice and bigotry in modern America.'"[63] In the court's view, "the use of race, in and of itself, to choose students simply achieves a student body that looks different. Such a criterion is no more rational on its own terms than would be choices based upon the physical size or blood type of applicants."[64] Conversely, within color blindness or formal-race discourse, to judge persons "without regard to race" is to judge persons on the basis of socially relevant or meritocratic criteria, or to judge them "as individuals." On this view, "individuals" possess skills and talents and diverse forms of cultural literacy, and any of these features may legitimately form the basis for rational or meritocratic judgments about them.[65] Color blindness discourse views these various socially relevant properties of individuals (including even certain aspects of their accent and appearance) as distinct and distinguishable from "race" as such. Thus, the *Hopwood* court reasons that "while the use of race *per se* is proscribed, state-supported schools may reasonably consider a host of other factors — some of which may have some correlation with race — in making admissions decisions."[66]

Within color blindness discourse, the concept of the "individual" does two kinds of work. The discourse of individualism signifies a particular kind of claim about race-neutrality, referring to those characteristics of persons apart from their formal-race. This concept of neutrality, in turn, supports a particular view of distributive fairness: providing opportunities to persons "without regard to race," that is, on the basis of "merit" or "qualifications," "achieved" rather than "ascriptive" characteristics. It is crucial to note that, within color blindness discourse, the right to be treated as an "individual" entitles persons to protection from classification on the basis of *formal-race* only.[67]

---

63. *Id.* at 946 (quoting Richard A. Posner, "The DeFunis Case and the Constitutionality of Preferential Treatment of Racial Minorities," 1974 *Sup. Ct. Rev.* 1, 12).

64. *Id.* at 945.

65. *See supra* text accompanying notes 6–7.

66. *Id.* at 946.

67. The objection to classifying persons on the basis of group membership pertains to

It is understood to be the essence of meritocratic rationality, or so-called equality of opportunity, to classify persons with respect to "socially relevant characteristics" which are taken as goods, or proxies for goods, in themselves. Thus, the *Hopwood* opinion deems it an affront to meritocratic ordering to take into account Cheryl Hopwood's race, but perfectly reasonable to discount her grade point average by taking into consideration the fact that she attended a community college and a state university.[68] Indeed, on this understanding of "equality of opportunity," it is the essence of "individualism" to categorize persons and to discriminate among them on the basis of such "socially relevant characteristics." Meritocratic social ordering celebrates this

---

classifications on the basis of formal-race only. Consider this typical objection to affirmative action: "If race should be the basis for the allocation of society's goods and opportunities, and if racial groups matter more than individuals, then we must accept affirmative action as it has evolved, even if such acceptance requires us to jettison the best in the American tradition. Race cannot serve this purpose, however, because the mere fact of a person's race is morally uninteresting." Terry Eastland, "The Case against Affirmative Action," 34 *Wm. & Mary L. Rev.* 33, 46 (1992); *cf.* William W. Van Alstyne, *Affirmative Action and Racial Discrimination Under Law: A Preliminary Review in Selected Affirmative Action Topics in Employment and Business Set Asides: A Consultation/Hearing of the United States Commission on Civil Rights* 181 (1985) ("Individuals are not merely social means; i.e., they are not merely examples of a group, representatives of a cohort, or fungible surrogates of other human beings; each, rather is a person whom it is improper to count or to discount by race." Quoting John E. Morrison, "Colorblindness, Individuality, and Merit: An Analysis of the Rhetoric against Affirmative Action," 79 *Iowa L. Rev.* 313, 326 n.93 [1994]).

68. *See* Lani Guinier, "The Real Bias in Higher Education," *N.Y. Times,* June 24, 1997, at A19 ("Had opponents of affirmative action looked beyond race to see why Ms. Hopwood was not admitted, they would have discovered that she lost points because she went to a community college and a state university. The University of Texas penalized Ms. Hopwood, who grew up under difficult circumstances and worked her way through school, because she graduated from a less competitive but more affordable college."); Siegel, "Colorblind Constitutionalism," *supra* note 20, at 35–36 (noting that opinion "throws racial discrepancies in admissions ranges into stark relief, while treating as equitably inconsequential the variance in admissions opportunities produced by the school's policy of favoring residents and its practice of weighting grades in accordance with the reputation of undergraduate institutions, despite its predictably class salient impact on admissions.").

kind of group-based discrimination and sees the "individual" as socially realized through it.[69] Persons talking about individualism and equality of opportunity in this way often depict the market, at least if constrained by color blindness principles, as a race-neutral mechanism of distribution; on this view, market rationality institutionalizes racial justice.[70]

Color Blindness as a Method of Characterizing Practices:
The Example of Griggs
Bearing in mind the highly specialized ways in which color blindness discourse reasons about race discrimination, race neutrality, and the traits of individuals and groups, we can now examine how color blindness discourse is employed to characterize particular social practices. We start with the paradigm case of overt racial segregation. In *Griggs v. Duke Power Co.*,[71] for example, the defendant originally placed all of its black employees in one department, called the "labor department," which had the lowest-paying jobs in the company.[72] Title VII, of course, outlawed practices employing such group-categorical racial distinctions as discriminating on the basis of race—that is, as irratio-

---

69. To appreciate how restrictive the use of "individualism" is in meritocratic claims about race, try substituting anything understood to be a socially relevant trait for the "formal-race" term in the quotation from Richard Posner that I discuss *supra* text accompanying note 63. For example, " 'The use of a[n] [educational degree or test score] to establish a presumption that the individual also possesses other, and socially relevant, characteristics, exemplifies, encourages, and legitimizes the mode of thought and behavior that underlies most prejudice and bigotry in modern America.' "

70. *See, e.g., supra* text accompanying notes 6–7. For two variants of this argument, compare Morris B. Abram, "Affirmative Action: Fair Shakers and Social Engineers," 99 *Harv. L. Rev.* 1312, 1326 (1986) ("As fair shakers see it, removing all barriers to the exercise of civil and political rights and to an individual's ability to participate in the free market system is the best possible way to promote justice"), with Richard A. Epstein, *Forbidden Ground: The Case Against Employment Discrimination Laws* 59–78 (1992) (arguing that eliminating constraints on market ordering will eliminate invidious race and sex discrimination). For a critical evaluation of such arguments, see Cass R. Sunstein, "The Anticaste Principle," 92 *Mich. L. Rev.* 2410, 2413–19 (1994) (evaluating arguments for and against view that free markets eliminate race and sex discrimination).

71. 401 U.S. 424 (1971).

72. *See id.* at 426–27.

nally treating applicants for employment on the basis of group membership rather than evaluating their merits as individuals. On the effective date of Title VII, the defendant moved to comply with the statute by eschewing use of group-categorical racial distinctions, and by requiring instead that all new applicants to formerly white departments would have to have a high school diploma or certain test scores.[73] Black applicants then challenged these new employment criteria as violating Title VII.

The district court ruled that by instituting these requirements the defendant did not discriminate on the basis of race.[74] It is easy to see how this argument runs. The company complied with Title VII by abandoning group-categorical racial distinctions and adopting instead group-salient employment criteria. In requiring a high school diploma or certain test scores as a condition of employment in its formerly all-white departments, the company was asking for qualifications that could well be relevant to employment, even if such traits were distributed through the population in a group-salient way. Thus, within a conventional understanding of color blindness, these new requirements were race-neutral, because they were not race-categorical even if they were race-salient.[75] Further, within a conventional understanding of color blindness, the new requirements treated applicants for employment as individuals because the requirements did not distinguish among applicants by racial group, but instead by traits of potential social relevance, even if these "meritocratic" criteria in turn rested on group-based generalizations about the aptitudes and abilities of the individual applicants who possessed them. As the district court observed,

The two tests used by the defendant were never intended to accurately measure the ability of an employee to perform the particu-

73. See id. at 427–28.

74. See Griggs v. Duke Power Co., 292 F. Supp. 243 (M.D.N.C. 1968).

75. Cf. id. at 248. The district court stated that: "In providing for prospective application only, Congress faced the cold hard fact of past discrimination and the resulting inequities. Congress also realized the practical impossibility of eradicating all the consequences of past discrimination. The 1964 Act has as its purpose the abolition of the policies of discrimination which produced the inequities." Id.

lar job available. Rather, they are intended to indicate whether the employee has the general intelligence and overall mechanical comprehension of the average high school graduate, regardless of race, color, religion, sex, or national origin.[76]

In accordance with the conventions of color blindness discourse, the defendant company had thus adopted a race-neutral policy even if the policy continued to exclude most blacks from employment in the higher-paying departments of the company. As this example should illustrate, the conventions of color blindness discourse make it possible for this society to characterize practices that enforce racial stratification as the product of "race-neutral" and "nondiscriminatory" principles of social distribution. This is one way in which color blindness discourse rationalizes racial stratification.

Yet in *Griggs,* the Supreme Court did not accept the lower court's reasoning about the legality of the policy in question. Instead, the Court held that, under Title VII, an employer who adopted facially neutral rules (such as the requirement of test scores or a high school diploma) that had a disparate impact on protected classes might still be found to discriminate on the basis of race, unless the employer could demonstrate some business necessity or justification for using the challenged criteria.[77] A particular understanding of race animates the Court's decision: The *Griggs* opinion points to the history of racially segregated education in the South to illustrate why the use of formally race-neutral criteria might nevertheless be discriminatory or unfair.[78] Given the unequal distribution of educational opportunity to blacks and whites, employment criteria associated with educational attainment would predictably select among applicants in a race-salient way and so reproduce and perpetuate distributive inequities between blacks and whites. *Griggs,* in short, recognizes what Gotanda calls "historical-race," discussing race as a social field of distributive injustice (in this instance, involving discriminatory or unequal educational opportunity).

76. *Id.* at 250.
77. See *Griggs,* 401 U.S. at 436.
78. See *id.* at 430 ("Because they are Negroes, petitioners have long received inferior education in segregated schools.").

Yet at the same time that the *Griggs* Court begins to discuss race in this thicker, "historical" sense, as arising out of the unequal distribution of socially valuable and relevant opportunities (such as education), the opinion simultaneously retains and deploys the discourse of individualism associated with formal-race, as it insists that (1) individuals have merit and qualifications independent of their racial identity; and (2) distributive fairness consists in distributing opportunities on the basis of these race-neutral traits. Mid-course in the opinion, "race" shifts semantic registers, transformed from a thick bundle of socially relevant traits back to a thin, socially irrelevant trait, when the Court observes that "Congress has not commanded that the less qualified be preferred over the better qualified simply because of minority origins. Far from disparaging job qualifications as such, Congress has made such qualifications the controlling factor, so that race, religion, nationality, and sex become irrelevant."[79] Thus, even as *Griggs* seemingly recognizes that race is a social formation, it reverts to the discourse of formal-race to assert that market rationality is race-neutral and institutionalizes racial justice. These unannounced discursive shifts are common in the case law and sustain the rhetorical power of color blindness discourse.[80]

Analyzed from this standpoint, color blindness discourse is a highly specialized mode of characterizing social practices. Consider again the logic of this semantic code in action. Since implementation of federal employment discrimination laws, employers rarely organize the workplace in overtly race-categorical terms. When plaintiffs challenge a seemingly race-salient practice as covertly race-based, a characterization dispute ensues along the lines we have just explored. Only if the evidence seems to support a narrative about the practice as covertly employing group-categorical racial distinctions (that is, irrational judgments based on "racial prejudice" that by definition serve no socially relevant end and function only to differentiate employees on the basis of formal-race) is the practice judged race-based; if the practice can be explained with respect to any socially relevant end, trait, or purpose,

---

79. *Id.* at 436.
80. *See, e.g.,* sources cited *supra* note 50.

it will be characterized as race-neutral, however race-salient in social incidence the practice might be. So, for example, suppose an employer interviews two black applicants and eight white applicants and hires a white employee; has he made an employment decision on the basis of race? A fact-finder would have to examine the evidence and character-ize the challenged decision as one that was race-neutral because based on socially relevant criteria ("qualifications," however race-salient in character or distribution they might be) or as one that was race-based (meaning that the fact-finder was willing to interpret the evidence as supporting a particular narrative in which the employer would refuse to hire any black applicant simply "because" that applicant was black, i.e., for no socially relevant reason other than prejudice.) [81]

81. Here, once again, the law generally assumes that the irrational, class-based animus would be directed at *all* class members indiscriminately. *See, e.g., Jeffries v. Harris County Community Action Ass'n,* 615 F.2d 1025, 1030 (5th Cir. 1980) ("Where both the person seeking to be promoted and the person achieving that promotion were women, 'be-cause the person selected was a woman, we cannot accept sex discrimination as a plau-sible explanation for [the promotion] decision.'" (quoting *Adams v. Reed,* 567 F.2d 1283, 1287 [5th Cir. 1978]) (holding that where both applicant promoted and applicant re-jected were black, challenged decision could not have resulted from race discrimination; reaching this result by following reasoning of sex-discrimination case); *cf. supra* text at notes 33–36 (discussing the ways law has characterized policies concerning pregnancy and grooming codes). Intermittently, however, the law does recognize that discrimina-tion could manifest itself in the act of differentiating among class members. Doctrine, however, typically reaches this result by recognizing subclasses within the targeted class and treating discrimination directed against members of such subclasses as actionable. *See Walker v. IRS,* 713 F. Supp. 403 (N.D. Ga. 1989) (dark-skinned African American em-ployee may bring Title VII action for discrimination based on darkness of skin because Title VII provides employees protection from discrimination based on "color" as well as "race"); *Jeffries,* 615 F.2d at 1032–35 (observing that "sex-plus" cases provide support for view that "disparate treatment of a subclass of women could constitute a violation of Title VII" and recognizing "black females as a distinct protected subgroup for purposes of the prima facie case and proof of pretext").

The bizarrely abstract conception of discrimination on which such doctrines are based is part of the formal-race discourse discussed in the text. As we have seen, the law generally defines discrimination as the cognitive error or irrationality that occurs when a decision maker differentiates among persons based on formal-race; on this view discrimination involves a misascription of traits, either (1) the assumption that formal-race (or "race per se") has any social relevance, or (2) the failure to recognize that indi-

Assuming the fact-finder decided that the employer had made the hiring decision on race-neutral grounds (i.e., on the basis of qualifications), plaintiffs would then, of course, have the option of challenging the "facially neutral," race-salient practice on disparate impact grounds; if the defendant employer could then demonstrate business

---

vidual members of a group may possess instrumentally relevant traits that most group members lack.

Sometimes, however, the law seems to acknowledge that discrimination involves more than a simple breakdown of instrumental rationality and verges on recognizing discrimination as a problem concerning status conflicts among groups involving the distribution of a society's material and dignitary goods. On this account the cognitive error of discrimination involves giving credence to particular narratives that justify policies and practices that unequally distribute social goods. When law proceeds from this intuition, doctrine treats discrimination/stereotyping as something more than the failure to recognize that individual members of a group may have different traits than those generally possessed by group members. On these occasions, the law treats discrimination/stereotyping as a normative, narrative process that involves morally suspect prescriptions and cognitively suspect rationalizations that together justify keeping certain groups in "their proper place." From the standpoint of this sociohistorical and narratological view of discrimination—which approaches the problem of race or sex discrimination as one involving the preferential treatment accorded members of some race/sex groups over others—the law is more adept at recognizing certain reasons for excluding some (although not all) group members as suspect rationalizations or stereotypes. In short, from this standpoint, the legal system recognizes as suspect the claim that particular blacks are lazy—or that particular women are too aggressive.

For a case caught between these two views of discrimination, see Price Waterhouse v. Hopkins, 490 U.S. 228 (1989) (reviewing refusal to promote female employee to partner in accounting firm on grounds that she was too aggressive and had interpersonal difficulties in dealing with staff). In Price Waterhouse, the plurality opinion first defines discriminatory animus as a distinction on the basis of formal-sex: "In saying that gender played a motivating part in an employment decision, we mean that, if we asked the employer at the moment of decision what its reasons were and if we received a truthful response, one of those reasons would be that the applicant or employee was a woman." Id. at 250 (plurality opinion) (note omitted). The plurality opinion then immediately proceeds to discuss discriminatory decision making in terms of the concept of "stereotyping": "We are beyond the day when an employer could evaluate employees by assuming or insisting that they matched the stereotype associated with their group.... An employer who objects to aggressiveness in women but whose positions require this trait places women in an intolerable and impermissible Catch-22: out of a job if they behave aggressively and out of a job if they don't. Title VII lifts women out of this bind." Id. at

necessity—that is, characterize the practice as serving some socially relevant, if race-salient, end—the employer's decision will once again be characterized as race-neutral within the usages of formal-race discourse as *Griggs* has elaborated them.

In a world where no signs identify practices that are "race-based," characterization of contested practices will play a crucial role in the operations of antidiscrimination law. Plainly, in such a world, fact-finders will have considerable latitude in explaining whether practices "discriminate" "on the basis of race." But before we even consider the ancillary racial assumptions that might inform exercise of that interpretive discretion, it is crucial to consider the limited nature of the claim antidiscrimination law makes when the law announces that a practice does not discriminate "on the basis of race."

Color Blindness Discourse and Claims of Distributive Justice

When the law announces that a practice does not discriminate on the basis of race, it speaks within the usages of formal-race discourse. In its original historical context, this familiar mode of talking about race made sense in debates over distributive justice in ways it no longer does today. As we have seen, formal-race discourse tells a particular story about practices that overtly classify on the basis of race; it deems such

---

251. For the *Price Waterhouse* plurality, does Title VII merely proscribe judgments on the basis of formal-sex? Or, does the statute proscribe stereotyping, considered as the failure to recognize that the individual plaintiff might have an instrumentally valuable trait (aggressiveness) that most other members of her class lack? Or, does the statute instead proscribe a variant of sex-plus, the refusal to hire an aggressive woman for a job that requires aggressive behavior, so that failure to hire a part of the class is tantamount to a refusal to hire all of the class, the "intolerable and impermissible Catch-22" to which the plurality opinion refers? The *Price Waterhouse* opinion understands that the refusal to promote an aggressive woman represents a prescriptive judgment that plays an important role in sustaining sex discrimination, but it is never confident in explaining how or why this is so. This confusion is evident in the way that the opinion characterizes the case as presenting a problem of "mixed-motive" discrimination. *See id.* at 234–36 (identifying as illegitimate ground of decision overtly sex-based comments about plaintiff's "aggressiveness" and as "legitimate" ground of decision putatively gender-neutral judgments about deficiencies in plaintiff's "interpersonal skills" in dealing with staff members).

practices instrumentally irrational (because the mere color of a person's skin can have no social relevance) and distributively unjust (because the belief on which such practices are predicated—that the mere color of a person's skin has social relevance—is the product of irrational racial prejudice). The claim that "race has no social relevance" can be understood, historically and contextually, as repudiating the relevance claims of status-race talk; and, when understood in this way, the claim that "race has no social relevance" is, of course, rich with meaning. But to observe as much is to recognize that the meaning of formal-race discourse arises in an act of negation, as formal-race discourse repudiates the particular set of practices and justifications associated with status-race discourse.[82] Once antidiscrimination law prompts the removal of "whites only" signs from institutions and practices, however, the claims of formal-race discourse begin to function somewhat strangely as a framework in which to evaluate the distributive justice of the practices that remain. This problem arises because of the usages of formal-race discourse itself. Formal-race discourse defines race in ways that are deeply at odds with the understandings of race that would seem to be relevant to evaluating the justice of our distributive practices.

Consider again how color blindness discourse understands the term *race*—as a group-categorical distinction that has no social relevance. In debates over the justice of our distributive practices, it might make symbolic or expressive sense to assert that race has no social relevance; but this claim about race, once disassociated from the historically specific practices and rhetorics it originally sought to contest, is not a sen-

---

82. As we have seen, formal-race talk takes its normative orientation from a particular sociohistorical project—the disestablishment or alleviation of racial stratification—during a period when racial stratification was enforced by a particular set of practices (employing group-categorical distinctions) that were in turn rationalized by a particular set of justifications (asserting the social relevance of race). Standing alone, formal-race talk quite self-consciously offers no social account of race apart from the claim that race has no social, political, or moral relevance. But if we reflect on the semantic structure of this claim, we can see that its (highly specialized) social meaning arises in the negation of another set of claims about race. Differently put, the claim that race has no social, political, or moral relevance derives all of its social, political, and moral valence in the repudiation of the particular social, political, and moral account of race offered by status-race discourse (i.e., claims of "prejudice," "racism," or "white supremacy").

sible way of talking about race if we mean to evaluate the justice, fairness, or distributive neutrality of particular practices that are alleged to discriminate on the basis of "race." To begin thinking about whether a particular practice might be just or fair with respect to matters of "race," it would seem that we would have to analyze "race" as it is manifested in a given society at a particular juncture of history: that is, to consider race as a social formation—like ethnicity and gender, arising out of the unequal distribution of socially salient traits across populations, or more dynamically, as a group-status relation arising out of the interaction of social structure and social meaning.

Yet as soon as we begin such a discussion, we will depart from the specialized assumptions about race on which formal-race talk is premised. Current scientific and social-scientific accounts of race do not treat race as a group-categorical distinction but instead conceptualize race in terms of group-salience—as arising out of the uneven incidence of genetic or phenotypic or social traits in a population;[83] this is the ap-

83. The Supreme Court intermittently analyzes race in this way, as do an increasing number of scholars. See, e.g., Saint Francis College v. Al-Khazraji, 481 U.S. 604, 609 n.4 (1987) (discussing biological and anthropological studies supporting view that "racial classifications are for the most part sociopolitical, rather than biological in nature"; noting that literature contends that "genetically homogeneous populations do not exist and traits are not discontinuous between populations; therefore, a population can only be described in terms of relative frequencies of various traits [and] clear-cut categories do not exist"); Anthony Appiah, "The Uncompleted Argument: Du Bois and the Illusion of Race," in "Race," Writing, and Difference 21, 30–32 (Henry Louis Gates Jr. ed., 1985) (discussing genetic studies demonstrating "extent to which members of . . . human populations we call races differ more from each other than they do from members of the same race"); Ian F. Haney Lopez, "The Social Construction of Race: Some Observations on Illusion, Fabrication, and Choice," 29 Harv. C.R.-C.L. L. Rev. 1, 10–16 (1994) (same); id. at 7 (describing race as "a vast group of people loosely bound together by historically contingent, socially significant elements of their morphology and/or ancestry, . . . a sui generis social phenomenon in which contested systems of meaning serve as the connections between physical features, races, and personal characteristics").

   Genetic and cultural accounts of race can be expressed in homologous terms, as arising out of the distribution of traits in a population. On this view, cultures are populations marked by distributions of relatively similar norms and understandings. Cf. Balkin, Cultural Software, supra note 56, at 49–50, 53, 90–97 (observing that cultures and subcultures are distributions of relatively similar shared understandings and habits). These traits, norms, and understandings are, of course, embedded in social relations

proach to race reflected in historical-race and culture-race discourses. Further, historical-race and culture-race discourses understand race as aggregations of *socially relevant* traits — that is, they conceptualize race as made of norms, understandings, cognitive and practical skills, material resources, life experiences, practices, activities, memories, concerns, commitments, fears, interests, desires, and identifications that are distributed in a society in group-salient patterns that persist with variable intensity over time. Some version of this approach to conceptualizing race as a social formation seems inevitable in debates over the justice of our distributive practices, however complexly we model the problem in institutional, dynamic, economic, or other terms. For if we want to identify particular social practices that are distributively just with respect to race, it would indeed seem that, whatever our view of distributive fairness, we would have to reason about race as it is *socially* instantiated, whether in historical or cultural terms.

By contrast, when antidiscrimination law reasons in terms of formal-race, the law defines discrimination with respect to a very specialized notion of race — race understood as a subgroup of the population marked by no traits of any social relevance. Once race is defined this way, any practice that can be characterized as rationally selecting for a socially relevant trait can be characterized as neutral with respect to race: that is, *as differentiating on the basis of some trait other than race itself.* But, of course, the "race" with respect to which the practice is said to be neutral is something of a legal fiction, in the sense that this usage of the term *race* arises out of special mode of talking about race (formal-race) that insists that race is a group-categorical distinction that has no social relevance.

---

and social structures that play an important part in making them meaningful. Contemporary theorists emphasize the dynamic interplay of social structure and social meaning in constructing race. *See also* Haney Lopez, *supra* at 7 (asserting that race "is neither an essence nor an illusion, but rather an ongoing, contradictory, self-reinforcing process subject to the macro forces of social and political struggle and the micro effects of daily decisions"). *See* generally Omi and Winant, *supra* note 32 (rejecting the view that race has a biological foundation and the view that it is merely a social "illusion" or cognitive error; adopting "racial formation" approach that understands race as growing out of interaction of "both social structure and cultural representation").

Our analysis of *Griggs* demonstrated just how limited color blindness talk is as a framework for reasoning about the justice of distributive practices in matters of race. In *Griggs*, as we saw, the Court relinquished the premises of formal-race discourse to reason about race as it is socially embodied in history. From this sociohistorical standpoint, the Court recognized that race is a site of unequal distribution of socially valuable (i.e., relevant) educational resources. Once the Court began to reason about race and education this way, it tacitly acknowledged that making judgments about the socially relevant traits of "individuals" involves making judgments within, not without, the social field of race.[84] Yet, precisely as *Griggs* verged on recognizing this fact, the opinion repressed the recognition by urgently reinvoking the premises of formal-race discourse and asserting that hiring criteria that select for traits that are relevant to the achievement of business purposes are distributively neutral with respect to race.[85]

Thus, as our analysis of *Griggs* demonstrates, the vice (or virtue) of color blindness discourse is that it conceals the distributive consequences of group-salient practices in a semantic code that defines instrumentally rational utterances as race-neutral. As antidiscrimination law tells the story, we never even have to face the question of reconciling conflicts between equality and efficiency goals, because formal-race discourse draws on concepts of instrumental rationality as a framework in which to define distributive justice in matters of race. Since Tussman and tenBroek began reasoning about race discrimination as a breach of instrumental rationality[86]—an approach that was in turn embedded in the foundations of strict scrutiny doctrine[87]—the law has

---

84. This would seem to follow, so long as we can identify no relevant distinction between the traits that are said to constitute individuals (as they appear in the particular bundles we call persons) and the traits that are said to constitute groups (as they appear in the particular distributions that give groups their distinguishable social "identities").

85. As *Griggs* triumphantly concludes, "Congress has not commanded that the less qualified be preferred over the better qualified simply because of minority origins. Far from disparaging job qualifications as such, Congress has made such qualifications the controlling factor, so that race, religion, nationality, and sex become irrelevant." *Griggs v. Duke Power Co.*, 401 U.S. 424, 436 (1971).

86. *See supra* note 53 and accompanying text.

87. *See id.* (discussing legal-process approaches to antidiscrimination law).

defined practices that can be characterized as selecting for traits that are instrumentally related to the achievement of legitimate social ends as practices that do not discriminate on the basis of race. In so doing, antidiscrimination law has defined distributive fairness in matters of race in terms of a specialized concept of race—formal-race—that, by definition, has no connection to those social features of race (whether historical or cultural) that might bear on the justice of our distributive practices.[88]

Yet the system of characterization employed by antidiscrimination law has been used by courts to designate a wide variety of race-salient practices as race-based, even when such practices are not identified by a sign reading "whites only." It has also been employed by courts to characterize a wide variety of race-salient practices as race-neutral, even when such practices are justified in the semantic code that has grown up in our civil rights culture to enable whites who understand themselves to be race-egalitarians to continue arguing about race relations without speaking in race-categorical terms.[89] What exactly is driving these results?

Once "whites only" signs are removed, the power of color blindness discourse to disrupt or to rationalize social stratification at any given moment in history seems to depend, not on some Archimedean point of race-neutrality that the discourse of color blindness identifies, but

88. When discrimination and neutrality are defined with respect to formal race, this highly abstract account of race will efface structural inequality in baselines and norms that shape meritocratic competition. Formal-race discourse does not register (1) inequality in the resources with which members of different groups can compete, or (2) the group-salience of traits deemed relevant to success in any given social undertaking, a form of bias often attributable to the group affiliation of those who originally defined how a task was to be performed, or to status-marking of the traits themselves (i.e., leadership requires "aggression" rather than "sensitivity," "initiative" rather than "responsiveness").

89. *Cf.* Siegel, "Equal Protection," *supra* note 20, at 1135–48 (demonstrating how prevailing definitions of discriminatory purpose insulate practices that are highly race- and gender-salient from legal challenge, with special attention to questions of crack cocaine and domestic violence); *see also supra* notes 32–33 and accompanying text (discussing how linguistically competent social actors are aware of the differences between group-categorical and group-salient distinctions and can manipulate them when discussing matters implicating race and gender relations).

rather on independent views about the nature of race held by those who wield the discourse. Differently put, those who embrace color blindness norms also hold beliefs about the nature of race as a social formation, and, in various doctrinal contexts, those concurrent convictions about the *social* nature of race play an important role in determining whether, and to what extent, claims about color blindness tend to undermine or legitimate social stratification.

If one assumes that, absent discrimination, members of different racial groups are relatively similar in their interests and abilities, then one would expect to find a relatively similar distribution of different groups throughout various fields of social endeavor; if, on the contrary, one assumes that there are significant and lasting differences among such groups, then one would expect to find an unequal distribution of the groups throughout the society. During the first decades of the Second Reconstruction, it was often assumed that differences in the social distribution of racial groups were largely attributable to the effects of present or past discrimination.[90] Since the 1970s, however, a growing body of scholars has drawn on ethnicity theory to attempt to explain social stratification as a product of group cultural dynamics rather than "discrimination." As Nathan Glazer and Daniel Moynihan explained in their introduction to a book on ethnicity in 1975: "Ethnic groups

90. For an illustration of how the interpretive presumptions of antidiscrimination law used concepts of discrimination to explain disparities in racial representation, *see,* for example, *International Brotherhood of Teamsters v. United States,* 431 U.S. 324 (1977). In the case the Court stated that statistics can be an important source of proof in employment discrimination cases, since "absent explanation, it is ordinarily to be expected that nondiscriminatory hiring practices will in time result in a work force more or less representative of the racial and ethnic composition of the population in the community from which employees are hired. Evidence of long lasting and gross disparity between the composition of a work force and that of the general population thus may be significant even though . . . Title VII imposes no requirement that a work force mirror the general population." *Id.* at 340 n.20; *see also* Vicki Schultz, "Telling Stories about Women and Work: Judicial Interpretations of Sex Segregation in the Workplace in Title VII Cases Raising the Lack of Interest Argument," 103 *Harv. L. Rev.* 1750, 1771–75 (1990) (discussing race discrimination cases decided between 1967–71 that explained the dearth of minority applicants for particular jobs in terms of a "futility" doctrine that interpreted the employment preferences of minority applicants in light of the exogenous—and racially discriminatory—norms and practices that might have shaped them).

bring different norms to bear on common circumstances with conse-
quent different levels of success — hence *group* differences in status."[91]
This social-scientific examination of the traits that might account for
the success and status of ethnic (i.e., "outsider") groups offered a new
way of talking about the relation of group difference and group stratification — one that self-consciously distinguished itself from the traditions of status-race talk and explained differences in the social position
of groups as arising out of *group-salient* distributions of traits in a population; consequently, this approach allowed for discussion of group difference and group status on terms that could be reconciled with the
central tenets of formal-race talk. Indeed, the race-as-ethnicity story
did more than offer a way of talking about group difference and group
status that was consistent with the central tenets of color blindness discourse; it coupled the story about individualism told by formal-race
talk with culturally potent narratives about the immigrant's struggle
from rags to riches that played an important role in redefining the
sociopolitical salience of color blindness discourse in politics and law.

Since the 1970s, assumptions about race-as-ethnicity have increasingly structured arguments about the moral grounds for and proper
application of antidiscrimination law in popular, academic, and, ultimately, legal fora.[92] Consistent with their origins in a theory of social

91. Nathan Glazer and Daniel P. Moynihan, "Introduction," in *Ethnicity: Theory and
Experience* 17 (Nathan Glazer and Daniel P. Moynihan eds., 1975), quoted in Omi and
Winant, *supra* note 32, at 31.
92. It would be a much longer story to trace how this mode of reasoning about race
infiltrates and begins to reshape antidiscrimination law during the 1970s and 1980s, af-
fecting interpretive presumptions concerning the ways one proves an individual dispa-
rate treatment claim and a pattern or practice claim, see, e.g., *Hazelwood Sch. Dist. v.
United States,* 433 U.S. 299 (1977), as well as the disparate impact claim, *see Watson v.
Fort Worth Bank & Trust,* 487 U.S. 977 (1988); *Wards Cove Packing Co. v. Atonio,* 490
U.S. 642 (1989), and the debate over racial quotas that culminated in the Civil Rights
Act of 1991.
The race-as-ethnicity story also played a rich and complicated role in the retrench-
ment of affirmative action law, starting with Justice Powell's compromise reformulation
of educational affirmative action as serving "diversity" rather than remedial ends in
Bakke, 438 U.S. 265 (1978). *See* Siegel, "Colorblind Constitutionalism," *supra* note 20, at
40–41. "Diversity" supplied a socially compelling rhetoric for educational affirmative
action precisely because the race-as-culture concept appealed to those who wanted to

stratification, these race-as-ethnicity arguments most frequently view race as manifesting itself in *socially relevant, group-salient* differences — a narrative frequently invoked to explain persisting social stratification in a society committed to meritocratic, individualist, and color-blind principles of distribution.[93] Infused with this specially coded narrative

---

affirm racial identity as something other than the accretion of historical injustice — as well as those, such as Justice Powell, who wanted to resist demands for racial redistribution justified by historical-race discourse or to dilute the authority of such collective-memory narratives by surrounding them with competing historical narratives of difference and disadvantage. *See id.; see also* Siegel, "Collective Memory," *supra* note 20, at 136–37 (noting that Justice Powell's claim that "we are a Nation of minorities" repudiates collective responsibility for racial stratification "by deconstructing the category of white persons understood as decendants of slave-owners"). Soon thereafter, the race-as-ethnicity narrative began to play an important role in affirmative action law outside the educational context, when the Court invoked culture-race discourse as a reason for intensifying the evidentiary showing that state actors would have to make to demonstrate they were entitled to adopt an affirmative action program for purposes of remedying past discrimination. *See* Siegel, "Colorblind Constitutionalism," *supra* note 20, at 43–46 (discussing cases such as *City of Richmond v. J. A. Croson Co.,* 488 U.S. 469 [1989]).

Finally, it bears noting that during the 1980s, these same currents were working themselves out in matters of sex discrimination law as well, most prominently in the debate provoked by the *Sears* case and "choice" or difference-based justifications for gender disparities in the work force. *See EEOC v. Sears, Roebuck & Co.,* 839 F.2d 302 (7th Cir. 1988). *See generally* Schultz, *supra* note 92 (discussing lack-of-interest arguments in sex discrimination cases).

93. *See, e.g.,* Nathan Glazer, *Affirmative Discrimination: Ethnic Inequality and Public Policy* 62–63 (1975) (arguing that antidiscrimination law erroneously assumes that, absent discrimination, there would be random distribution of women and minorities in all jobs, when the distribution of jobs among minority groups is best explained by differences in educational qualifications, regional variables, and difficult to quantify factors "such as taste or, if you will, culture"); Abram, *supra* note 70, at 1315–16 ("Because groups — black, white, Hispanic, male, and female — do not necessarily have the same distribution of, among other characteristics, skills, interest, motivation, and age, a fair shake system may not produce proportional representation across occupations and professions, and certainly not at any given time. This uneven distribution, however, is not necessarily the result of discrimination. Thomas Sowell has shown through comparative studies of ethnic group performance that discrimination alone cannot explain these ethnic groups' varying levels of achievement.").

In a recent attack on the Civil Rights Act of 1964, Charles Murray offered an instance of this equality-of-opportunity/equality-of-results argument that is particularly trans-

about race-as-ethnicity—*a narrative that would seem to be interested in cultural accounts of race only insofar as the "culture" concept provides an explanation, and justification, for social stratification*—antidiscrimination law can become a powerful tool for rationalizing social inequality. For once formal-race talk is coupled with this highly specialized form of culture-race talk, the particular version of color blindness discourse that results will begin to interpret existing distributions as evidence of the outcomes that result when "individuals" and the groups to which they belong are given "equality of opportunity." Discrepancies in the rates at which different groups participate in various fields of social endeavor no longer seem to be the product of present or past discrimination;[94] instead discrepancies in the rates at which different groups participate in various fields of social endeavor will appear as evidence of the differing distribution of group-salient traits that mark and define racial (or ethnic or gender) groups as culturally distinct groups. From this same standpoint, any attempt to vary the rate at which different groups participate in various fields of social endeavor will appear as a

---

parent in its assumptions about the "real" nature of race and gender differences: "At any moment in history a completely fair system for treating individuals will produce different outcomes for different groups, because groups are hardly ever equally represented in the qualities that go into decisions about whom to hire, admit to law school, put in jail, or live next door to . . . [A] system that . . . judg[ed] each case perfectly on its merits [] would produce drastically different proportions of men and women hired by police forces, blacks and whites put in jail, or Jews and gentiles admitted to elite law schools." Charles Murray, *What It Means to Be a Libertarian: A Personal Interpretation* 85–86 (1997).

The Supreme Court would seem to have adopted some (presumably more temperate) version of this social hypothesis to discredit the presumption that the discrepant representation of minority groups is likely attributable to discrimination, and disparages assumptions about "proportional representation" to justify, *inter alia,* constitutional restrictions on affirmative action. *See* Siegel, "Colorblind Constitutionalism," *supra* note 20, at 57–61 (analyzing racial commitments of color-blind constitutionalism). *See* generally *id.* at 54 ("A story about competition among groups with different genetic and cultural endowments explains, and justifies, relations of racial status; a story about maintaining appropriate distinctions between public and private spheres explains, and justifies, legal rules that preserve relations of racial status.").

94. *Cf. supra* note 90 and accompanying text (discussing presumptions of race discrimination jurisprudence during the 1960s and 1970s).

breach of distributive neutrality and an inefficient and unjust form of "social engineering."[95]

Yet, as should be plain by now, the only way that such accounts can demonstrate that existing discrepancies in group participation result from the workings of equality of opportunity (rather than discrimination) is by asserting beliefs about race-as-ethnicity—that is, by describing race as manifested in the unequal distribution of socially relevant traits throughout the population.[96] As Charles Murray succinctly puts it: "At any given moment in history a completely fair system for treating individuals will produce different outcomes for different groups, because groups are hardly ever equally represented in the qualities that go into decisions about whom to hire, admit to law school, put in jail, or live next door to."[97] In short, the claim that race neutrality is served by embracing principles that secure "equality of opportunity" rather than "equality of result" turns out to rest on independent social assumptions about the nature of race that flatly contradict the premises of color blindness discourse itself. Such arguments nicely demonstrate my earlier point that formal-race discourse, standing alone, does not supply a basis in which we can cogently debate the justice of our distributive practices; to enter such a debate, one has to make certain claims about the nature of race as a social formation—that is, to begin to talk about race as it is manifested in a particular society at a particular juncture of history. This color blindness discourse cannot do, unless those employing formal-race talk overtly or covertly couple this mode of reasoning about race with modes of reasoning about race that are rooted in historical-race or cultural-race discourse.

To summarize the argument as I have developed it thus far, color blindness discourse in antidiscrimination law is a mode of character-

95. *See supra* note 93 (discussing interpretive presumptions of culture-race discourse as elaborated during the last several decades).

96. This observation addresses the debate as it unfolds in the political arena, where too often "discrimination" and "culture" are treated as distinct and opposing, rather than interlocking and mutually constitutive, social processes that might cause discrepancies in the rates at which members of different groups participate in various fields of social endeavor.

97. Murray, *supra* note 93, at 85.

izing social practices that specifies whether such practices distribute access to social goods in legitimate ways; it works both to discredit and to rationalize practices that maintain social stratification. Because color blindness discourse defines "discrimination on the basis of race" in highly specialized ways—as a practice of group-categorical differentiation that serves no instrumentally relevant end—color blindness discourse can both discredit and rationalize practices that perpetuate racial stratification.

Formal-race discourse originated in the effort to explain why practices that overtly segregated on the basis of race were instrumentally irrational and distributively unjust. Once antidiscrimination law used formal-race discourse to eliminate practices that overtly classified on the basis of race, the rhetoric of formal-race discourse took on a new life. Because formal-race discourse defines race as a group-categorical distinction having no social relevance, formal-race discourse can now be used to characterize as race-neutral any race-salient practice that can be described as instrumentally related to the achievement of a legitimate social end. But such practices are only neutral with respect to a highly restrictive definition of race—race understood as a form of group categorical distinction that has no social relevance. This highly formalized mode of characterizing practices conflates claims about the instrumental rationality of practices with claims about the distributive justice of practices; claims about the distributive justice of practices generated within this formal-race framework are unpersuasive precisely because race has been defined as a trait that has no social relevance—an understanding of race that would seem entirely unsuited to deciding whether practices are distributively just with respect to race. As we examine the application of antidiscrimination law and the political debates it has engendered, it would appear that the power of color blindness discourse to disrupt or to rationalize social stratification does not flow from the ability of formal-race discourse to identify some ground of distributive neutrality in social practices, but instead reflects assumptions about the nature of race as a social, historical, or cultural formation that are independent of—and in conflict with—the formal premises of color blindness discourse itself.

"Preservation-through-Transformation": Antidiscrimination and Antisubordination Principles in Sociohistorical Perspective

To this point I have tried to show how the concept of stratification missing from Post's sociological account of the field enables us to make
more sense of the trope of blindness at the heart of antidiscrimination
law. In the preceding part of my response, I showed how color blindness discourse relates social structure and social meaning in such a way
as to disrupt racial stratification and to rationalize it. In concluding
my response, I now want to give this argument temporal extension,
to consider its implications given the ways that practices and meanings which sustain group inequality evolve as they are contested over
time. I believe that a sociological approach that is attentive to stratification and the mutability of status-enforcing practices can teach us much
about the changing sociopolitical salience of color blindness discourse
over the course of the Second Reconstruction, and in so doing, shed
new light on the debate between antidiscrimination and antisubordination norms that currently divides academic and popular opinion
about matters of race and sex equality.

As I take up these questions, I will be reflecting once again on what
it means to do antidiscrimination law from a sociological standpoint,
and so returning to the main challenge of Post's essay. First, and perhaps most significant, I will argue that a sociological approach attentive
to stratification and to the mutability of status-enforcing practices can
in fact tell us more about the underlying purposes of antidiscrimination law than Post's lecture suggests. When we consider how tropes of
blindness have been deployed from a sociohistoric vantage point, we
can see that a commitment to alleviating stratification is and has been
central to the project of antidiscrimination law since the beginning of
the Second Reconstruction. But, I argue, the very method of analysis that demonstrates the centrality of this normative commitment to
the antidiscrimination project simultaneously reveals the limitations of
meta-principles (such as antidiscrimination or antisubordination) in
guiding our critical practices. Thus, in the final analysis, I concur with
Post that a sociological approach to the field constructively reframes
many important normative questions, yet does so without rendering

them amenable to resolution by application of general principles alone. I reject the legal-formalist assumption that abstract ("principled") reasoning alone can adduce the kinds of social groups toward which discrimination is directed or the kinds of social forms it assumes. However much such understandings may be informed by principle, they are forged in history, through social struggle, as various features of social stratification are contested over time.

To resume consideration of some of the larger methodological questions raised by Post's essay, I would like to begin this last part of my response as I intend to end it: by pausing to consider reflexively where we stand as we comment on the nature of antidiscrimination law. In his essay, Post characterizes the alternative perspective he offers on antidiscrimination law as "sociological"; at various points I have characterized my own style of analysis as "sociohistorical." Each of us is nevertheless doing "law" — endeavoring to step outside doctrinal frameworks of analysis to make observations about the operations of law that we understand as deeply pertinent to the development of the law, and ultimately, to the formulation of doctrine itself. Indeed, it seems to me that this effort to break out of legal categories and apprehend the "real" and "actual" operations of law in society is a characteristic feature of legal reason, one familiar way in which members of a legal order contest its governing rules and norms. In such struggles, doctrine typically is denounced as overly if not perniciously formalistic, and legal decision makers are urged to take actual social practices and understandings into account in reshaping the law. This impulse may assume the form of a self-conscious jurisprudential movement, such as Legal Realism, or a call for interdisciplinarity within law, such as Sociological Jurisprudence or Law and Economics. Or, this impulse may manifest itself interstitially, as an appeal to common social understanding that appears in the course of ordinary legal argument. For example, many of the most famous rhetorical assaults on Jim Crow are appeals for legal doctrine to take account of what "everyone knows" about the "real meaning" of segregation.[98] Indeed, as we consider the rhetorical form of such in-

---

98. *Plessy v. Ferguson*, 163 U.S. 537, 557 (1896) (Harlan, J., dissenting); *cf.* Charles L. Black Jr., "The Lawfulness of the Segregation Decisions," 69 *Yale L. J.* 421, 424 (1960)

terpretive conflicts, we can see eerie parallels between Justice Harlan's passionate challenge to legal formalism and indignant protests about the meaning the Court has given "equal protection" today.[99]

Since the delegitimation of Jim Crow, appeals for antidiscrimination law to take into account social structure and social meaning typically occur within two areas of doctrine: in debates about the legality of "group-conscious" remedies that differentiate among individuals on the basis of group membership, and in debates about the legality of "facially neutral" practices that differentially burden groups without formally differentiating among their members. Doctrinal debate occurred in these areas because, as my analysis of *Griggs* shows, by the 1970s civil rights law had precipitated a shift in the rule structure and justificatory rhetoric of the practices that enforced the differential social status of racial groups.[100] With the enforcement of civil rights law during the 1950s and 1960s, those whites interested in preserving racial stratification began to abandon the use of overt group-categorical distinctions, more or less at the same time as those interested in using civil rights law to *alleviate* racial stratification began to employ practices incorporating

---

(responding to the claim that segregation treats the races " 'equally' " with the suggestion that "we ought to exercise one of the sovereign prerogatives of philosophers — that of laughter"). In *Brown,* the Court avoided this kind of appeal to common social understanding by invoking social-scientific evidence about the harms of segregation in the opinion's predictably criticized "footnote 11." *See Brown v. Board of Educ.,* 347 U.S. 483, 494 n.11 (1954).

99. Consider Justice Harlan's demand in *Plessy* for the Court to take account of what "everyone knows" about the "real meaning" of segregation, 163 U.S. at 557, and the challenge to legal formalism that drives Justice Stevens's dissent in *Adarand Constructors v. Pena,* 515 U.S. 200 (1995), in which Justice Stevens argued, "The Court's explanation for treating dissimilar race-based decisions as though they were equally objectionable is a supposed inability to differentiate between 'invidious' and 'benign' discrimination. . . . But the term 'affirmative action' is common and well understood. Its presence in everyday parlance shows that people understand the difference between good intentions and bad." *Id.* at 245 (Stevens, J., dissenting); *see also id.* ("The consistency that the Court espouses would disregard the difference between a 'No Trespassing' sign and a welcome mat. . . . An interest in 'consistency' does not justify treating differences as though they were similarities.").

100. *Cf. supra* text accompanying notes 25–27 (discussing the preservation-through-transformation dynamic).

group-categorical racial distinctions.[101] Under these circumstances, the doctrinal injunction against discrimination — with its account of blindness understood as a prohibition on group-categorical race and sex distinctions — seemed to point equality law in directions at odds with the intuitions of many civil rights advocates interested in ameliorating the persisting inequality of traditionally disempowered groups.

In 1976, Owen Fiss engaged these debates about the legality of "benign" racial distinctions and facially neutral practices in an influential article that appeared in *Philosophy & Public Affairs* entitled "Groups and the Equal Protection Clause."[102] He opened his argument with an appeal for law to free itself from the constraints of antidiscrimination doctrine and renew itself by once again examining the social relationships it was endeavoring to shape. As Fiss defined his project:

> I want to suggest that the antidiscrimination principle embodies a very limited conception of equality . . . [and] to outline another mediating principle — the group-disadvantaging principle — one that has as good, if not better, claim to represent the ideal of equality, one that takes a fuller account of social reality, and one that more clearly focuses the issues that must be decided in equal protection cases.[103]

The "group-disadvantaging principle" that Fiss proposed in 1976 is often referred to as an "antisubordination principle," an "antisubjugation principle," or an "anticaste principle," and especially as elaborated by Catharine MacKinnon,[104] Derrick Bell, Laurence Tribe, Charles Lawrence, Randall Kennedy, Ruth Colker, Cass Sunstein, Kenneth Karst,

---

101. *See* Siegel, "Equal Protection," *supra* note 20, at 1141–44.

102. Owen M. Fiss, "Groups and the Equal Protection Clause," 5 *Phil. & Pub. Aff.* 107 (1976).

103. *Id.* at 108.

104. MacKinnon was the first to give an extended, particularized, and critically provocative explication of the antisubordination approach in her influential analysis of sexual harassment. *See* Catharine A. MacKinnon, *Sexual Harassment of Working Women* (1979) [hereinafter MacKinnon, *Sexual Harassment*]; her subsequent elaboration of the theoretical framework of this path-breaking work has been equally influential in the antidiscrimination literature. *See* Catharine A. MacKinnon, "Difference and Dominance: On Sex Discrimination," in *Feminism Unmodified* 32 (1987).

and many others, has played a central role in the equality literature,[105] particularly in debates over affirmative action and doctrines concerning discriminatory purpose and disparate impact.[106]

I was fortunate to study equality law with Owen Fiss, as did Robert Post before me, and my approach to equality law has, from the outset, been profoundly shaped by the antisubordination literature: by the quest to understand antidiscrimination law in light of social structure and social struggle, as involving problems in group inequality. Yet I was never drawn to the project of philosophically elaborating an antisubordination principle as such. Perhaps because of our common training in American literature and history, I share with Post a skepticism that law can be fruitfully articulated in principles that can be abstracted from the concrete social practices law aspires to shape.[107] It is for this reason that I have attempted to analyze questions of gender and race inequality in a "thick" sociohistorical framework, examining the institutions, practices, stories, and meanings through which group stratification has been maintained, with special attention to the ways in which such institutions, practices, stories, and meanings have evolved through periods of social conflict. Indeed, one reason that I have engaged in this project of thick description is to show how the antisubordination principle can be understood as an appropriate ex-

105. See, e.g., Laurence H. Tribe, American Constitutional Law § 16–21, at 1514–21 (2d ed. 1988); Ruth Colker, "Anti-Subordination above All: Sex, Race, and Equal Protection," 61 N.Y.U.L. Rev. 1003 (1986); Kenneth L. Karst, "The Supreme Court, 1976 Term — Foreword: Equal Citizenship Under the Fourteenth Amendment," 91 Harv. L. Rev. 1 (1977); Randall Kennedy, "Persuasion and Distrust: A Comment on the Affirmative Action Debate," 99 Harv. L. Rev. 1327 (1986); Charles R. Lawrence III, "The Id, the Ego, and Equal Protection: Reckoning with Unconscious Racism," 39 Stan. L. Rev. 317 (1987); Sunstein, supra note 70, at 2410.

106. See, e.g., Siegel, "Reasoning from the Body," supra note 20, at 369 n. 426 (citing commentators who have employed antisubordination values "to distinguish between benign and invidious race- and sex-based state action, as well as to criticize doctrines requiring a showing of discriminatory purpose to challenge facially neutral state action").

107. For one account of Post's views on these matters, see Robert Post, "Recuperating First Amendment Doctrine," 47 Stan. L. Rev. 1249, 1272–73 (1995) (arguing that "law . . . does not deal with values as merely abstract ideas or principles"; instead, "all legal values are rooted in the experiences associated with local and specific kinds of social practices").

pression of antidiscrimination commitments in sociohistorical, rather than philosophical, terms.[108]

My work illustrates how struggles over group inequality can transform the rules and reasons by which social stratification is enforced and justified. This dynamic, which I call preservation through transformation,[109] suggests why the debate between antidiscrimination and antisubordination principles transpired during the 1970s. As civil rights advocates challenged the conventional practices and rationales supporting race and gender inequality, they precipitated a shift in the rule structure and justificatory rhetoric of these status regimes. In time, an antidiscrimination principle that had been elaborated with respect to the status-enforcing practices and rationales of the early twentieth century became ill-suited for challenging the kinds of status-enforcing practices and rationales that emerged in their wake.[110] It is in this context that we can understand Fiss's call in 1976 for a new "mediating" principle through which to interpret the Equal Protection Clause.

Considered from this sociohistorical vantage point, we can understand Fiss as expressing the normative commitments of the "Second Reconstruction" in rhetorical terms that might enable continued critical engagement with the world the civil rights movement brought into being. That world was one in which—thanks to color blindness discourse—many of the traditional practices and rationales supporting race and gender inequality were discredited; yet it was also a world in which—again, thanks to color blindness discourse—stratification by race and gender persisted across social sectors, often enforced in new ways and rationalized in new rhetorical terms. As *Griggs* illustrates, in this world, social stratification was commonly sustained through "facially neutral" practices, rather than group-based classifications, whereas group-based classifications were more commonly

108. *See* generally Siegel, "Equal Protection," *supra* note 20 (analyzing contemporary equal protection doctrines in long-term historical perspective); *cf.* Siegel, "Colorblind Constitutionalism," *supra* note 20, at 57–61.

109. Siegel, "Rule of Love," *supra* note 20, at 2175–88 (describing dynamic of preservation-through-transformation).

110. *Cf. id.* at 2188–96 (discussing gender cases); Siegel, "Equal Protection," *supra* note 20, at 1141–48 (discussing race cases).

employed to alleviate social stratification than to entrench it.[111] Fiss's "group-disadvantaging principle" thus began the work of translating the status-disestablishing commitments of the Second Reconstruction into rhetorical terms better adapted to challenging the status-enforcing practices of the civil rights era. In this universe, the discourse of anti-subordination identified and critically illuminated the social practices supporting race and gender stratification in ways that, *Griggs* notwithstanding, the discourse of antidiscrimination and color blindness no longer could.[112]

On this account, then, Fiss and those who followed him sought a new language in which to describe the assault on racial stratification *already* initiated during the Second Reconstruction in the language of color blindness itself. If I am correct in this account, then it would appear that sociohistorical analysis enables us to say considerably more about the purposes of equality law than Post has. Throughout his lecture, Post suggests that a sociological understanding of antidiscrimination law would have us reshape race and gender conventions so as to promote the purposes of the law. But he never gives any hint as to what those purposes might be. By contrast, on my account, the purpose of anti-discrimination law is and has been to ameliorate certain forms of racial group stratification. At the height of the civil rights movement, the discourse of antidiscrimination and color blindness constrained certain practices used to enforce racial segregation and to this extent served to alleviate group inequality. In other words, at the beginning of the Second Reconstruction, the discourse of "antidiscrimination" promoted what we might now understand as "antisubordination" ends. Clarify-

111. *See id.*

112. *Cf.* Siegel, "Colorblind Constitutionalism," *supra* note 20, at 56 (arguing that the sociopolitical salience of color blindness discourse varies with the historical context in which it is invoked). Color blindness discourse was rhetorically designed to delegitimate the group-categorical classifications of status-race discourse as status-race discourse stood at the beginning of the Second Reconstruction. As I have demonstrated (*see supra* text accompanying notes 65–69), it protected persons from no other form of group-based categorization, as it entitled persons to be treated as "individuals" with respect to their formal-race only. So, given particular social practices to which it was responsive, color blindness discourse ameliorated racial group stratification; that is, it worked to alleviate the subordination of African Americans as a group.

ing this much about the moving commitments of the Second Reconstruction seems to me of absolutely crucial consequence, given the very
different racial views and commitments of those who now claim Martin
Luther King Jr.'s legacy.[113]

Of course, in King's era, application of antidiscrimination principles
only partly disestablished group stratification; nor is it clear that many
of the white Americans who applied such principles ever aspired to
more.[114] No doubt in this social struggle, as in so many others, Americans differed in their understanding of the kind of changes it would
take to realize the ideal of equality in social practice, and just as important, they differed in the degree to which they imagined that a world of
race and gender equality would nonetheless remain race- and gender-
stratified.[115]

Indeed, if we consider the question at this level of specificity, I agree
with Post that a sociological approach still requires close and context-
based analysis of the purposes of antidiscrimination law before it can
be translated into legal doctrine. To see why, let us turn from the problems of positive to normative analysis, that is, from historical reconstruction to present prescription. Suppose we embrace an antisubordination principle. On what grounds do we decide which practices inflict
dignitary harm? Any expression of sexuality in the workplace? If not,
which expressions of sexuality, and why? How much differentiation on
the basis of race or gender should survive in a race- and gender-equal

113. For illustrations of the ways that opponents of affirmative action invoke the mantle
of the civil rights movement of the 1950s and 1960s, see Siegel, "Rule of Love," *supra*
note 20, at 2185 n.244. For an analysis of the social vision and normative understandings informing equality rhetoric in debates over the Civil Rights Act of 1964, *see* Drew
Hansen, "Civil Rights and the Making of the American Ideal, 1954–1964" (unpublished
manuscript, on file with author).

114. *See, e.g.,* Siegel, "Colorblind Constitutionalism," *supra* note 20, at 57–61; Siegel,
"Equal Protection," *supra* note 20, at 1142–43.

115. This is exactly the problem we confront if we want to give any more precise and
positive account of the heterogeneous commitments of civil rights advocates during the
1950s and 1960s. This was an era in which advocates spoke a language of blindness and
individualism that worked to alleviate racial group stratification but that may have ob-
scured, possibly from the advocates themselves, divergent visions of the kind of social
world that tropes of color blindness might bring into being.

world? And in which social contexts? In the family setting? In matters of erotic attraction? In the world of work? Politics? War? Even if we say that antidiscrimination law has as its purpose the disestablishment of entrenched forms of group inequality, or the amelioration of social stratification, or the general end of eliminating the unjust subordination of traditionally disempowered groups, there obviously remains ample ground for disagreement in a variety of social contexts about the particular ends we are seeking, the best means of achieving them, and, finally, the kinds of group life that amelioration of social stratification will support. In short, the very method of analysis that demonstrates the centrality of antistratification concerns to the antidiscrimination project simultaneously reveals the limitations of "meta-principles," such as "antidiscrimination" or "antisubordination," in guiding our critical practices.

Once we understand equality and discrimination as problems in group stratification produced and rationalized by an ever-changing array of social practices and meanings, the question of our ends becomes far more complicated to articulate. As I have explored with respect to nineteenth-century conflicts over women's rights, attempts to imagine status-equality inevitably draw on the status values of the very social order they aspire to disestablish.[116] But the practices and meanings con-

116. See Siegel, "Home as Work," *supra* note 20, at 1131–35 (exploring how the joint property claim advanced by the nineteenth-century woman's rights movement transvalued gender conventions, drawing on aspects of separate spheres discourse even as it was contesting it); *id.* at 1198–1205 (demonstrating how the movement's new conception of economic equality — avoiding domestic labor in favor of wage work outside the home — internalized status norms about work rooted in relations of gender, race, and class inequality).

Of course, the tendency of emancipatory discourses to imagine equality in ways that tacitly incorporate the status values of the culture they are criticizing has been the subject of much recent commentary in the critical race literature. *See, e.g.,* Angela Harris, "Race and Essentialism in Feminist Legal Theory," 42 *Stan. L. Rev.* 581 (1990); *see also* Wendy Brown, *States of Injury: Power and Freedom in Late Modernity* (1995) (examining how resistance discourses and oppositional projects can incorporate discourses and values of the world they mean to subvert). Those who would employ an emancipatory discourse always must be interrogating that discourse in an attempt to ascertain whether its vision of equality rests on the value systems of an unjust status hierarchy. In particular, members of subordinated groups who may simultaneously occupy positions

stituting the contested status order are always in flux, and so inevitably will be emancipatory efforts to imagine and express status-equality. Hence, during the 1970s we witnessed a revolt against color blindness talk as an "assimilationist" rhetoric that tacitly encoded white privilege, and a corresponding effort to embrace "diversity" talk and to affirm the dignity of subordinated groups by contesting directly the traditional status-valuation of their social and cultural traits. Race — that is, membership in a subordinated racial group — was no longer something that had to be politely overlooked, but instead emerged as a social fact about which members of subordinated groups could express pride. Second-wave feminism began in this blindness tradition as well, with equality initially expressed in terms of the flight from motherhood, and then slowly reformulated into a demand for enhanced valuation of the institution, values, and work of nurturance, a dignitary claim that was almost immediately interrogated as a suspect form of "essentialism."[117] The movement for gay pride has similarly reappropriated and transvalued identity discourses and practices once only contemptuously referred to by the epithet "queer."

In short, discourses about subordination and equality set up a rhetorical framework in which we are continuously arguing about the ways human dignity is expressed in a given social order. The abstract language in which we express our principles or purposes can only point us to a question whose concrete resolution has to be fought out in the field of social life, with respect to a variety of different structures and

---

of privilege in other status orders must be vigilant in avoiding what I call "positional bias," or expressions of dignitary harms or movement goals that reflect the social experience and concerns of the subordinated group's more socially privileged members. "Essentialism" arising out of this kind of positional bias is in all likelihood unavoidable and just as inevitably will and should be challenged with the ongoing contestation of social hierarchy. But the kind of essentialism I call reification — treating historically or circumstantially contingent aspects of group experience as relevant to the articulation of equality goals — seems to be an inevitable, and even necessary, part of the emancipatory project, so long as generalizations about the socially specific circumstances and traits of the subordinated group are treated as contingent and revisable. See Siegel, "Home as Work," supra note 20, at 1211–17.

117. See id.

meanings. It seems to me uncontrovertible that at any given moment of history, members of a society will experience many questions of status inequality, such as slavery or lynching, as relatively uncontroversial. Yet there are bound to be others about which there is deep social dissensus, such as "date rape," "meritocratic standards," or the ways we value child care. These controverted questions about the justice of our social practices set up a normative struggle about which there may or may not ever emerge wide-ranging social consensus. In short, there are many unanswered questions nested in the general commitment to ameliorate unjust forms of group-based stratification or subordination, perhaps as many unanswered questions as are nested in the commitment to color blindness. Posing these questions in more concrete sociohistorical terms can fruitfully inform debate and focus dispute about them without necessarily resolving the matters in issue.

This is no doubt why Post suggests that the ends of judicial accountability and doctrinal coherence would be served by adoption of a sociological approach to the field.[118] As my own work suggests, I am simultaneously compelled by such claims and yet despairing of them. Fundamental questions concerning the distribution of dignitary and material goods are at stake in disputes over antidiscrimination law. For just this reason the capacity of a sociohistorical or sociological approach to clarify positive and normative dimensions of the equality question may, in certain contexts, prove to be a liability as well as a virtue. For example, even if the "dominant approach" masks the actual operations of antidiscrimination law, judges and other legal decision makers may not necessarily wish to unmask them. The antidiscrimination narrative is, after all, a story told by members of relatively privileged groups explaining why they are prepared voluntarily to divest themselves of some of their status privileges. In a variety of circumstances, legal decision makers may not in fact wish to understand, acknowledge, or address the social dynamics that sustain the inequality of groups.[119]

118. *See* pp. 39–52.

119. I espouse no simple determinism here, but observe only the uncontroversial: Social interest and social position can play a role in predisposing decision makers, advocates, and scholars to certain views about the appropriate ends of law. *Cf.* Siegel, "Rule of

Implicit in the sociological approach is a second potential liability. As we have seen, when considered from a sociological standpoint, the disestablishment of group inequality is a messy affair. Once we abandon tropes of transcendence and understand that we are aspiring to destabilize the social salience of race and gender without eradicating it, it is not always clear what equality looks like or how we get there. Such ambiguities are at the heart of recent disputes over sexual harassment law and pornography. The antidiscrimination literature now contains much discussion of subordination, but less frequently acknowledges the kinds of controversies that may arise in determining how particular practices "subordinate," or why they do so.[120] To avoid the complex

---

Love," *supra* note 20, at 2180–81 (discussing how judges can interpret law "in good faith" while at the same time interpreting law in ways that reflect "selective sympathy and indifference" to certain social groups; observing that "sometimes . . . critical oblivion is bliss, especially when it is interest-convergent").

120. Catharine MacKinnon first elaborated an antisubordination framework in the course of demonstrating how sexual harassment was sex discrimination, and her book-length analysis of a subordinating practice remains a model in the field. *See* MacKinnon, *Sexual Harassment, supra* note 104, at 117 (arguing that courts should evaluate contested practices with a view to determining "whether the policy or practice in question integrally contributes to the maintenance of an underclass or a deprived position because of gender status" and supplying detailed account of how sexual harassment does so). As MacKinnon continued to explore how relations of subordination are enacted in different forms of heterosexual sexual practice, her work generated increasing controversy. *See, e.g., Pleasure and Danger: Exploring Female Sexuality* (Carole S. Vance ed., 1984); Kathryn Abrams, "Sex Wars Redux: Agency and Coercion in Feminist Legal Theory," 95 *Colum. L. Rev.* 304, 329–46 (1995); Harris, *supra* note 116, at 598–601; Robin L. West, "The Difference in Women's Hedonic Lives: A Phenomenological Critique of Feminist Legal Theory," 3 *Wis. Women's L. J.* 81 (1987). MacKinnon surely is not alone in offering a close analysis of how particular practices subordinate. *See, e.g.,* Charles R. Lawrence III, "If He Hollers Let Him Go: Regulating Racist Speech on Campus," 1990 *Duke L. J.* 431 (1990); Mari J. Matsuda, "Voices of America: Accent, Antidiscrimination Law, and a Jurisprudence for the Last Reconstruction," 100 *Yale L. J.* 1329, 1332 and n.10 (1991) (invoking methods of legal realism and sociology of law in analyzing accent discrimination); Siegel, "Reasoning from the Body," *supra* note 20 (offering historical and contemporary analysis of abortion and its regulation that demonstrates how social structure and social representation interact to construct and rationalize contested practice). However, literature in the field often employs the discourse of subordination without acknowledging the extent to which the project proposed involves this kind of contest-

and the contestable, both judges and advocates may shy away from discussing the kinds of interpretive and predictive judgments that support claims about equality and discrimination, sociologically conceived. In short, in our political culture, there are distinct advantages to maintaining the dominant conception. What tropes of blindness may lack in descriptive accuracy, they more than compensate for in familiar and uncontroversial rhetorical force.

Still, there is everything to be gained from wrestling with such large questions from a more particularized sociological standpoint, so long as we do so in full awareness of the positive and normative conflicts we are bound to encounter along the way. For it is in the crucible of contests such as these—high-stakes struggle at the intersection of social value and social practice—that a society continually revises its understanding of unjust status hierarchies and consequently opens its imaginative horizons to new forms of social ordering. So it is that this society has struggled, from generation to generation in times past, to reinvent itself in the more perfect image of its commitment to freedom and equality. And so it is that future generations of Americans will no doubt do so again.

Are there risks in taking this historicizing vantage point on the interpretive conflicts in which we will inevitably engage as we argue about how to vindicate our normative commitments in our social practices? Absolutely. Our political culture prizes rule-like simplicity in its standards and individualism in its principles; the critical project to which this lecture and response point promises neither. Neither Post nor I have attempted to package the inquiries we have undertaken in doc-

---

able theorization of particular practices. *Cf.* Colker, *supra* note 105, at 1066 (arguing antisubordination framework presents "hard questions that cannot be addressed theoretically"; the article "set[s] forth a principle and a framework under which we can begin to answer these questions" which can only be addressed "in specific factual settings"). For one unusually forthright encounter with the complexities of elaborating an antisubordination theory, see Tracy E. Higgins, " 'By Reason of Their Sex': Feminist Theory, Post Modernism, and Justice," 80 *Cornell L. Rev.* 1536, 1594 (1995) (urging the Court and feminist legal theorists to abandon arguments that "rely on prepolitical conceptions of gender difference" and "acknowledge the exercise of power that is implicit in their own efforts to represent women politically and linguistically").

trinal "bites." Indeed the sociological turn, at least as we each have explored it here, would seem to resist doctrinal assimilation precisely because it breaks from the ways that the dominant tradition has figured the meaning of equality for so many decades now.

But this seems to me as much a virtue as a vice. As one who read MacKinnon and Bell in delight at their refusal to engage debate on the terms law offered them, I want to defer conversation about exigencies of advocacy long enough to wrestle again with what we can fathom of the actual and the possible. For, as MacKinnon and Bell have so vividly demonstrated for us, if we can liberate the imagination from law, it is possible to enliven law with new imaginings. This, too, is doing law, for, in ways more various than we can know, our intuitions about the justice of our practices would seem to be narrative.[121]

What, for me, is at stake in this critical encounter with the past? For all the abstract argument of this essay, I might trace its roots to stories I was told as a child. My father first explained the civil rights movement, segregation, and slavery to me in terms of the post-Holocaustal injunction "Z'Chor," or remember. In his stories, the forms of human injustice were plural, particular, and incommensurable, yet illuminated each other in disturbing ways. As I can now see, the questions his seemingly simple stories raised for me then continue to haunt my work today.

What if it turns out that what matters most are the stories that shape our intuitions of the just and reasonable, intuitions that theory and doctrine then articulate as norms, principles, and rules? And what if one of the most compelling of those stories in antidiscrimination law today is a certain narrative of progress in which we stand as ethical sophisticates equipped with vision and virtue that distinguishes us from our more ethically primitive forebears? This story invites us to form our identifications and commitments by repudiating the past, but can prove problematic precisely as it does so. Knowing ourselves as unimplicated by the past invites the kind of complacency that deadens the instinct to introspection and action both.

Moved perhaps by certain stories of my childhood, in my writing

---

121. *See* Siegel, "Collective Memory," *supra* note 20; *see also* Balkin, *Cultural Software*, *supra* note 56, at 203–10.

I have worked to deflate the kind of confidence this narrative engenders, a kind of confidence that comes from mistaking hindsight for a moral virtue rather than a critical vantage point.[122] I have tried to decipher the past by asking, how are these ethically primitive forebears *my* forebears — that is, how might past generations of Americans have lived in worlds genealogically linked to or sociologically like my own? For me, asking such questions gives the practice of remembering both an ethical and a political dimension. No doubt, looking to the past and seeing continuity in the face of change can be sobering, even paralyzing; yet is it any more risky than looking to the past and seeing change in the face of continuity? As this nation's experience in recent decades illustrates, confidence in the redemptive possibilities of change can engender forms of self-satisfaction that may just as readily sap the collective will.

Without some awareness of our historical position, how are we to wield the rhetorical tools with which we reason about the justice of any community we might build? Even if this perspective on our project reveals that our tools are blunt and flawed, aren't we better off trying to find our way chastened by the knowledge that we, too, are fallible creatures whose principles and judgments are culturally contingent than in proceeding in willful disregard of that fact? Reckoning with our limitations need not involve relinquishing responsibility. Rather it presents us with a problem that is inescapably, perhaps even constitutively, human. As soon as a child has learned to say — "I did it," "He did it," and then "He made me do it" — she has learned how to represent herself in a discourse of causes and a discourse of effects. Henceforth, she has a choice, and with it, the narrative resources in which to construct a self as acting or acted on, agent, object, or any mix of the two. For all the sophistication she may thereafter acquire in representing herself to herself and to others, it is a choice that she can never again refuse.

122. *See* Siegel, "Equal Protection," *supra* note 20, at 1146–48.

Robert C. Post | Response to Commentators

Academic life contains few pleasures more intense than writing for an audience as astute and as generous as the four commentators to my essay. As this response demonstrates, I have learned much from them, particularly regarding the logical relationship between the dominant conception and the sociological account. What I chiefly wish to stress, however, is my deepest gratitude for their constructive and discerning insights.

Tom Grey, for example, makes an excellent and useful point about the potential tension between the rule of law and what I call in my essay the "sociological account."[1] Grey is entirely correct to stress that the insights yielded by a sociological apprehension of antidiscrimination law could encourage overly ad hoc and contextualized judgments, which the internal morality of the law ought properly to resist.

This tension between contextualism and formal consistency, however, is not entirely new to the law, and we are not without mechanisms for its ameliorization. In tort law, for instance, where the common law seeks to reproduce the nuanced and individualized judgments charac-

---

1. Thomas C. Grey, "Cover-Blindness," reprinted in this volume, pp. 85–97.

teristic of community norms, we typically place decisions in the hands of a jury. Jury decisions are figured as "merely" factual and hence as outside of the rule of law. Juries are deliberately rendered nonaccountable and their decisions stripped of precedential force.

Yet tort law does not entirely abandon rule of law values, for judges, in the context of motions to dismiss or motions for judgment *non obstante veredicto* (NOV), can confine jury decisions within definite limits. Of course, judges must also instruct juries about the standards and criteria that ought to govern their deliberations, but judicial instructions are usually phrased at a level of generality that adroitly reconciles contextualism with formal consistency.[2] We have developed a multitude of legal mechanisms, therefore, for negotiating the messy tensions usefully identified by Grey, and perhaps these mechanisms might also prove helpful in the context of antidiscrimination law.

I also entirely agree with Anthony Appiah's perception that judgments of equality and inequality must ultimately reflect a genuinely moral perspective capable of convincingly justifying the differential treatment of persons. I was particularly appreciative of Appiah's incisive parsing of the idea of a "stereotype." My own use of the word was relatively simple, resting on the elementary notion of generalization. The word *stereotype* originally referred to a printing process of mechanical reproduction invented at the end of the 1700s, but the *Oxford English Dictionary* reports that by the middle of nineteenth century the word had already acquired its contemporary meaning of "something continued or constantly repeated without change."

One advantage of hewing to this crude view of "stereotype" is that its very abstraction brings into view the connection between stereotypes and the conventions that underwrite the substance of social life. Stereotypes summon conventional regularities, without which human meaning would be impossible. To refer to an example mentioned at the outset of my essay, the only reason why Balzac could believe that the "mind of a man could be ascertained by the manner in which he holds his cane," is because of conventions, or stereotypes, linking patterns

2. *See, e.g.,* Robert C. Post, "The Social Foundations of Privacy: Community and Self in the Common Law Tort," 77 *Calif. L. Rev.* 957, 959–78 (1989).

of behavior with mental states. Without the proximate fixity of such stereotypes, social life would collapse into chaos.

That having been said, however, stereotypes, conventions, and generalizations can prove false and misleading, and it is therefore exceedingly useful for Appiah to distinguish among "statistical" stereotypes, "false" stereotypes, and "normative" stereotypes. His discussion reveals how these distinctions can clarify our apprehension of actual cases. My only reservation derives from the sense that sometimes the distinction between "statistical" and "normative" stereotypes does not inhere in the fact of the matter, but in its apprehension. Often when it is said that women are "weak" or that they lack "aggression," for example, it is not clear whether the assertions signify empirical, statistical claims, or whether they signify instead normative claims about what it means to be a woman.

Conventions can be simultaneously descriptive and normative. Stereotypes can also hover ambiguously between these meanings, sometimes assuming the status of empirical claims, and sometimes modulating into what Appiah elegantly terms "scripts for identities."[3] It is thus an achievement, for which Title VII law is partly responsible, to be able authoritatively to interpret many of these stereotypes as merely "statistical."

Judith Butler's response ably exposes and deepens many of the philosophical themes I had hoped to advance.[4] She ultimately raises the key question of how we can "account for the transformation of the stereotype within the practice of gender if there were not something else in gender, as it were, that is not immediately co-opted or foreclosed by the stereotype."[5] She worries that

> in claiming that race and gender are stable and systematic features of social reality . . . and in claiming that persons cannot

3. K. Anthony Appiah, "Stereotypes and the Shaping of Identity," reprinted in this volume, pp. 55–71.
4. The query that she puts to me—how to account for "those dimensions of personhood that do not, strictly speaking, appear"—is pertinent and important, and certainly beyond the confined scope of these comments. My guess is that I would want to think about such questions in roughly the way that Wittgenstein thinks about the issue of pain.
5. Judith Butler, "Appearances Aside," reprinted in this volume, pp. 73–83.

legibly appear to us without these conditions of social appearance in place, are we perhaps fortifying these categories precisely in their stereotypicality and persistence? By what means, then, are they disrupted and revised?[6]

These are exactly the right questions to ask, and they have no easy answers. In trying to understand them, I recur to the analogy of language. The meaning of words depends entirely on mutual conventions and shared understandings — "stereotypes," as it were. Yet these stereotypes do not prevent us from transforming language. We can forge new meanings and alter the conventions by which we script the world. We can speak poetry instead of prose. But even poetry is expressed within language; it successfully communicates only because it is always already situated within the conventions by which meaning as such is constituted.

It is in this sense that I believe that stereotypes "underwrite" the practice of gender. They do not exhaust the practice, because any given stereotype is susceptible to change and transformation, in exactly the way that the meanings of words are susceptible to change. But just as meaning remains necessarily conventional, so, too, altering stereotypes merely revises, rather than eliminates, the content of stereotypes.

Of course, gender or race could cease to be relevant categories, the way that serfdom has ceased to be a relevant category. But the category of serfdom vanished because the forms of life that made the category pertinent disappeared, and I doubt that there is any imminent likelihood of a similar social transformation about to overtake either race or gender. To the extent that these categories remain relevant, their meaning will be underwritten by the shared conventions, the stereotypes, that make social meaning possible. This will be true however successfully we seek to unsettle and revise the received meanings of these stereotypes.

It is possible, however, that Butler's worry may be directed not at the generic properties of social meaning, but rather at the specific account of law implicit in my essay. It is true that I speak of law as having specific, articulable purposes. It can fairly be said that I characterize the

6. See pp. 81–82.

law as speaking prose, rather than poetry. But this is because, as Robert Lowell writes, "the law is a sledgehammer, / not a scalpel."[7]

The law as an institution is a crude, blunt instrument of public policy. In part this is a consequence of the law's function, which is to coordinate the decisions of thousands of government officials and to direct the actions of millions of private persons. In part it is a consequence of the internal morality of the law; the rule-of-law values invoked by Grey point powerfully toward stability, predictability, and internal consistency. And in part it is a consequence of the fact that important aspects of antidiscrimination law are statutory, enacted by a legislature precisely to attain definite objectives.

These factors combine to push antidiscrimination law toward an internal organization that strives to accomplish discrete, relatively clear, articulated ends. As a practical matter, therefore, to speak of the efforts of antidiscrimination law to transform the practices of gender and race is to speak of its efforts to alter these practices from one form to another. The ends of antidiscrimination law can and should change over time, which in practice means that the law will unsettle and progressively revise these practices. But it is implausible to imagine the law in any given moment as pursuing anything other than specific objectives.

Of course, antidiscrimination law could take as its specific goal the radical suspension of the practices of gender and race, so as to reveal persons simply as persons. This may be what Butler has in mind when she speaks of "unsettling the social conditions by which persons become intelligible at all."[8] Surely Butler is right to stress this admirable aspiration. Although every person comes to us already enmeshed within the linguistic significations that define personhood, and to that extent always already caught within conventional understandings, we also know what it means to break through stereotypes to acquire a more immediate, vivid, and seemingly "truer" perception of a person.

But strange things happen to the law when it aspires to this condition. Something like this aspiration may well lie behind the trope of blindness that presently controls antidiscrimination law. What I at-

7. Robert Lowell, "Fetus," in *Day by Day* 34 (1977).
8. *See* p. 83.

tempted to demonstrate in my essay, however, is that this aspiration does not produce the kind of "unsettling" that Butler seeks; instead, it modifies conventions of race and gender in ways that are implicit and unconsidered. Because gender and race remain socially salient categories, and because they are likely to abide despite the best efforts of antidiscrimination law, the trope of blindness within law does not so much unsettle these practices as it redefines them.

I take this to be a central point of Reva Siegel's extensive response, which trenchantly argues that the trope of blindness does not transcend but instead actively entangles antidiscrimination law in the actual practices of race and gender.[9] Particularly illuminating is her discussion of the elastic and permeable ways in which contemporary antidiscrimination law classifies actions and rules as "based on" race or gender. These are significant doctrinal and ideological mechanisms by which antidiscrimination law regulates its own recognition of the manifold ways in which it intersects with the social practices of race and gender.

Siegel has written extensively and profoundly about the history of race and gender. I have learned much from her pungent and subtle accounts of the actual operation of antidiscrimination law. In her response, Siegel argues that race and gender must be understood as conditions of social stratification, and that antidiscrimination law has historically intervened to dismantle some, but not all, of these conditions. Through the trope of blindness, antidiscrimination law has paradoxically served to validate certain forms of stratification.

Siegel's argument seems to me largely correct, and I endorse it. But I would reserve three points of qualification. First, although the concept of stratification makes a great deal of sense within the core areas of race and gender, there are other areas of antidiscrimination law where the concept has less bite. The domain of religion, for example, is at least as venerable as those of race and gender, yet stratification does not seem a particularly useful way to understand contemporary American prohibitions against discrimination on the basis of religion. Appiah's

9. *See* Reva B. Siegel, "Discrimination in the Eyes of the Law," reprinted in this volume, pp. 99–152.

invocation of the problem of "bigotry"[10] seems more pertinent. This would also seem to be true with respect to other areas of antidiscrimination law, such as sexual orientation or Vietnam veteran status. There are still other areas of contemporary antidiscrimination law, however, such as age or marital status, where neither stratification nor bigotry seem especially relevant. Though stratification may be a useful frame for understanding important aspects of antidiscrimination law, therefore, it is not comprehensive.

Second, even within the core domains of race and gender, the concept of stratification may not exhaustively explain the operation of antidiscrimination law. Though I agree that the concept does illuminate exceedingly important dimensions of the relationship of antidiscrimination law to race and gender, there may remain other facets of this relationship that are not so centrally elucidated by the concept. Aspects of Title VII's upholding of conventional dress and grooming codes, for example, may be better explicable in terms of maintaining heterosexist norms than in terms of stratification between the sexes.

Third, and most important, Siegel's observations concerning stratification suggest an important ambiguity about what is meant by the "purpose" of antidiscrimination law. I should have stressed more clearly than I did in my original essay that the dominant conception and the sociological account are not symmetrical concepts. They cannot be substituted, one for the other. This is because the dominant conception expresses a moral vision that is internal to the law, while the sociological account represents an external account of the operation of law.[11] The dominant conception expresses a "purpose" of the law, but the sociological account does not.

As the work of John Rawls indicates, the trope of blindness has deep roots in contemporary theories of justice and of morality. If one were to ask a judge why the law ought to impose a regime of color blindness, she could reply that it was right and proper for the law to act in

---

10. *See* pp. 66–67.

11. For a discussion of the distinction between internal and external accounts of the law, *see* Neil MacCormick, *Legal Reasoning and Legal Theory* 275–92 (1978).

ways that render race invisible. The ideal of color blindness expresses a genuine moral commitment; it is neither a pretext nor a ruse. That is why the dominant conception functions, as Siegel accurately observes, affirmatively "to legitimate the distributive regimes that sustain group stratification."[12]

My critique of the dominant conception is that it contains an image of how antidiscrimination law works that systematically masks and distorts the true operation of the law. This observation is relevant to the question of whether the dominant conception represents a desirable or adequate ideal for antidiscrimination law. I proposed the sociological account to provide an external perspective that would make visible how antidiscrimination law actually functions, and in this way to reveal the inadequacies of the dominant conception. My suggestion was that we ought seriously to consider whether to refashion antidiscrimination law to pursue a different internal ideal, one that takes account of and that does not contradict the insights of the sociological account.

The sociological account cannot by itself provide such an ideal. Although the shift to an external perspective helps us better understand the true effects of our internal purposes, it cannot simply be substituted as an alternative internal ideal. If a judge were asked to explain her decisions, she could not respond that she was engaged in a social practice that modifies another social practice. A judge would instead have to articulate an internal justification for antidiscrimination law that was morally convincing, that acknowledged the actual interplay between such law and the social practices of race and gender, and that was defensible in terms of the particular requirements of legal doctrine. The Court's rationale in *Weber* of breaking down "old patterns of . . . segregation and hierarchy" might, for example, be a candidate for such a reformulated ideal.[13]

The objective for antidiscrimination law that the Court advances in *Weber* belongs to the class of proposed internal purposes that we would now call "antisubordination" theories. Siegel eloquently summons the historical genesis and normative attraction of these theories,

12. *See* p. 106.
13. *United Steelworkers of Am. v. Weber*, 443 U.S. 193, 208 (1979).

which challenge us to dismantle hierarchy, disadvantage, and subordination.[14] As I suggested in my essay, antisubordination theories do not seek to transcend history; they instead conceive law as an institution acting to modify other institutions. Unlike the dominant conception, therefore, they do not contradict the very premise of the sociological account.

But the sociological account is nevertheless relevant to the assessment of antisubordination theories. The power of such theories often flows from the implicit presumption that there exist independent metrics of hierarchy or disadvantage which it is the task of antidiscrimination law to equalize. We are sometimes told that the purpose of antidiscrimination law is to erase such differences in power or wealth as exist between races or sexes. Although there is surely some truth to this presumption, it is also the case that in its operation antidiscrimination law does not function in this purely redistributive fashion, even in the relatively progressive areas of disparate impact analysis and affirmative action.[15]

A sociological account would invite us to clarify how it is that antidiscrimination law actually does function. If it does not merely equalize predefined variables, like power, then what exactly does it do? It is evident, I think, that in many contexts antidiscrimination law seems as much concerned with defining what should count as hierarchy or disadvantage as it is with applying any antecedent metric. Antidiscrimination law postulates normatively acceptable social meanings for race and gender, and these meanings, in turn, color what we perceive as subordination. The area of sexual harassment law is a particularly fascinating venue for the study of this dynamic.[16] In such contexts, notions of hierarchy express conclusions about what the proper nature of these practices ought to be.

---

14. Siegel is, I think, correct to trace the normative structure of these theories to Fiss's "group-disadvantaging principle." Owen M. Fiss, "Groups and the Equal Protection Clause," 5 *Phil. & Pub. Aff.* 107, 108 (1976); Siegel, *supra* note 9, at 109–10.

15. *See, e.g.,* Barbara J. Flagg, "Fashioning a Title VII Remedy for Transparently White Subjective Decisionmaking," 104 *Yale L. J.* 2009, 2030–31 (1995).

16. For a fine discussion, *see* Katherine M. Franke, "What's Wrong with Sexual Harassment?," 49 *Stan. L. Rev.* 691 (1997).

This suggests that in many contexts "subordination" is a label that carries within it a normative account of race and gender. Most antisubordination theories are normative in this way. Although these theories may usefully suggest standards to assess the operation of antidiscrimination law, they do not explain how that law actually functions. Only a sociological account will offer such clarification. Only a sociological account will reveal the gap between the operation of antidiscrimination law and the normative goals implicit within antisubordination theories.

It is of course true that we should not set in stone whatever we might learn from a sociological analysis. Even if sociological inquiry demonstrates that antidiscrimination law is not presently redistributive, for example, we could change our purposes and hence transfigure the actual practices of antidiscrimination law. But surely an essential (if modest) first step in evaluating any such proposed changes would be to apprehend the nature of our own current commitments, as they stand revealed in the actual operation of our law. As Siegel's response and her historical work demonstrate, understanding the implicit vision of race and gender that underlies the present functioning of antidiscrimination law is a hugely complex and daunting task. If our capacity to achieve firm and enduring reform depends on the acquisition of self-knowledge, however, it is nevertheless a necessary task.

In this context, I would interpret Siegel's concept of stratification as an exceedingly useful amplification and elaboration of the sociological account. It offers a complex and systematic framework for apprehending the subtle ways in which antidiscrimination law modifies the actual practices of race of gender. It enables us to grasp in a deeper and more comprehensive way the impact of the dominant conception, and hence empowers us more accurately to evaluate that conception. But, like the sociological account, it is not itself an internal moral vision capable of guiding the law. As Siegel herself acknowledges, it is "messy" to apply the concept of stratification because "it is not always clear what equality looks like."[17]

In my essay, I deliberately bracketed the question of the internal

17. *See* p. 149.

principles that ought to guide antidiscrimination law. I instead offered the modest observation that there were important advantages to formulating these principles in a manner that was cognizant of the insights that an external perspective, like the sociological account, could bring to bear. Particularly in light of Appiah's and Siegel's responses, however, I should add that, whatever the substance of these principles, they ought to reflect genuine moral commitments. They ought to flow from a convincing social vision that identifies which aspects of the social practices of race or gender ought to be changed, and why. Although such principles would no doubt be strengthened if formulated in light of the insights provided by Siegel's concept of stratification, they cannot be reduced to that concept. Stratification is a term of descriptive analysis; it is not a moral purpose.

I suspect that if courts were to take seriously the insights of the sociological account, they would recognize that antidiscrimination law serves different purposes in different contexts. If one compares the role of stratification in gender and in sexual orientation, for example, it is evident that antidiscrimination law must combat very different social phenomena in these two domains. It is plausible to expect these differences to affect the moral vision pursued by the law. Grey perhaps puts the matter best when he notes that in articulating the objectives of the law, we ought to "take account of the nature of the enemy."[18]

18. *See* p. 92.

Contributors

K. Anthony Appiah is Charles H. Carswell Professor of Afro-American Studies and Professor of Philosophy at Harvard University.

Judith Butler is Maxine Elliott Professor in the Departments of Rhetoric and Comparative Literature and Chair of the Department of Rhetoric at the University of California, Berkeley.

Thomas C. Grey is Nelson Bowman Sweitzer and Marie B. Sweitzer Professor of Law at Stanford University.

Robert C. Post is Alexander F. and May T. Morrison Professor of Law at the University of California, Berkeley.

Reva B. Siegel is Nicholas deB. Katzenbach Professor of Law at Yale Law School.

Index

Affirmative action, 49–51, 57, 69–70, 97, 161–162

Antidiscrimination law: and autonomy, 45, 60–62; and doctrinal coherence, 43–47; dominant conception of, 21–22, 24, 25, 39–53, 74–75, 86; and functional rationality, 19–20, 24, 26–29, 31–36, 40–43; and individualism, 25, 29; and judicial accountability, 42–43; and legalism, 95–97; logic of, 1–2, 10–21; and privacy, 33–36, 60–61, 90; as purposive, 47–49, 153–154, 157; and the rule of law, 95–97, 153–154, 157; and sexual attraction, 30–31, 58–59, 68–69, 90; shaping the social practices of race, 48–49, 52, 59, 69, 89–90; shaping the social practices of gender, 34, 38–39, 47–49, 52, 59, 68, 70, 89–90, 157–58, 161; and social hierarchy and caste, 50, 87–89, 91–93, 94; and social practice, 22, 38–39, 42–43, 157, 160; and social stratification, 158–159, 162–163; sociological account of, 40–53, 153, 159–163; as transformative, 20–21, 24, 25, 32, 34, 39, 40, 47–49, 50, 82, 157

Antidiscrimination principle, 14

Anti-lookism, 2–3, 9–10, 32 n.115, 40 n.146, 48 n.168, 52, 85

Antisubordination, 41 n.147, 50, 70, 87–89, 92–93, 160–161

Appearance, 15, 36–39, 73–75, 76–81; as constitutive, 81; discrimination on the basis of, 9–10, 15, 31–32, 73; and functionalism, 76, 78; as social practice, 21–22; versus reality, 2, 3, 5, 86

Autonomy, 6–7, 45, 56, 60, 66

Balzac, Honoré de, 2

Bigotry, 8, 65–67, 85, 159

Blindness, 14–15, 20–21, 27–28, 40 n.146, 58, 66, 83, 86, 88, 91, 97, 157–160

Body Image Task Force, 2

Bona Fide Occupational Qualification (BFOQ), 17, 24–32, 34, 47 n.166, 48, 62, 63, 64, 90

Brest, Paul, 14

Cleburne v. Cleburne Living Center, Inc.,
12–13
Craft v. Metromedia, Inc., 31–32, 42, 70–71
Customer preferences, 26–36, 42, 45 n.164

Dignity, 11–14, 16, 19, 36 n.133, 60, 75, 83
Discrimination on the basis of: age, 93–
94; appearance, 9–10, 13, 15, 36–40, 48
n.168, 74–75, 82–83, 85–86; clothing,
6, 7, 31–32, 36–39, 90, 159; disability,
93–94; grooming, 6–7, 36–39, 43–47,
49, 90, 159; marital status, 11, 159; obesity, 11; race, 10, 13, 91–92; religion, 11,
158–159; sex, 10, 18–20, 23–39, 58–59,
92, 163; sexual orientation, 46 n.165,
93–94, 159, 163; tattoos, 6–7
Discriminatory purpose, 51, 62
Disparate impact, 14 n.51, 20 n.75, 51
n.181, 62, 161
Disparate treatment, 17, 57–59
Donohue v. Shoe Corp. of America, 13, 67
Dress regulations, 6, 7, 31–32, 36–39, 159

Egalitarianism, 57–58
Equal opportunity, 6, 9, 18, 25, 44, 88–89
Equal protection clause, 12, 17–18, 50–52
Equality, 4–5, 56–60, 70, 88; and dignity,
60, 75; as sameness, 56, 66

Fairness, 8–11
Fesel v. Masonic Home of Delaware, 33–36,
48, 60
Functional Rationality. *See* Instrumental
Rationality

Gender: and appearance, 78–79; and biology, 89–92; and grooming and dress
regulations, 36–39, 64–65; and privacy,
33–36; and separate spheres, 92; and
sexual attraction, 30–31, 58–59; as a
social practice, 21–26, 30–39, 45, 47–49,
58, 156; and stereotypes, 23–24, 28–30,
33–36, 79–80, 82, 155–156
Griffin v. Michigan Dept. of Corrections,
35–36, 61

Individualism, 25, 30, 32, 34–36, 46 n.165,
51, 61, 76; and appearance, 31–32, 36–
39; as "context-free," 25–26, 39; and
functionalism, 76; and privacy, 33–36;
and sexual attraction, 30–31
Individuality, 56, 60, 62
Instrumental Rationality, 5, 8, 10, 16–
21, 24, 75; and appearance, 37–38; and
blindness, 27–28, 42–43; as "context-
free," 19–21, 25–26, 39, 40; and customer preferences, 26–32; and discrimination, 19–20, 24, 26–28, 30, 40;
and the Kantian critique, 19, 75–76; as
socially embedded, 26–28
Intrinsic worth, 13, 14, 16, 19, 75–76, 83
Invidiousness, 58–59, 62, 89, 91, 93–94
Irrelevant characteristics, 5–6, 13

Job performance and discrimination,
5–6, 17, 19–20, 23–36
Johnson v. Transportation Agency, 50, 53
Juries, 154

Lam v. University of Hawaii, 13, 67
Lanigan v. Bartlett & Co. Grain, 37–38
Law as a social institution, 22, 25–26, 34,
42, 82, 87, 94–96, 156–157, 160–161
Legalism, 95–97

Merit, 13, 14, 16
Mill, John Stuart, 57, 68
Miss Lonelyhearts, 8–9, 58

Obesity, 11
Orchestra auditions, 18–21, 27
Original position, 15–16, 21, 22, 40, 41

Physical characteristics, 7, 8
Prejudice, 8–13, 15, 16, 19–21, 27, 39, 70
Price Waterhouse v. Hopkins, 13, 24, 46,
67
Privacy, 33–36, 60–61, 90
Public actions, 59–60, 69–70
Public rights, 61

Race as a social practice, 21–22, 48–49, 69, 89–92, 156

Rationalization, 19, 75–76

Rawls, John, 15–16, 159

Rule of law, 95–97, 153–154, 157

Santa Cruz ordinance, 2–10, 15, 40, 49, 52, 58, 65–66

Schaar, John, 18

Self-expression, 7, 45

Serfdom, 156

"Sex-plus" discrimination, 43–46

Sexual attraction, 30–31

Sexual harassment, 161

Sexual privacy, 61

Social hierarchies and caste, 50, 87–89, 91–94

Social phenomenalism, 78

Sociological account, 40–53, 153, 159–163

Sontag, Susan, 3

Stereotypes, 1, 13, 23–25, 29–36, 45–47, 50–51, 63, 66–67, 79, 82, 85–87, 154–157; and appearance, 31–32, 36–39; astereotypical, 80, 83; false, 64–65, 67, 155;

normative, 64–69, 155; and privacy, 33–36; as scripts for identities, 68, 155; and sexual attraction, 30–31; statistical, 63–67, 155

Stratification, 158–159, 162–163

Theory of Justice, 15–16

Title VII, 12–13, 17–18, 20 n.75, 23–39, 43–44, 46 n.165, 47 n.166, 48, 50, 67, 155, 159

TRB, 9–10, 40

United Steelworkers v. Weber, 50, 53, 57, 87, 160

Veil of ignorance, 15, 19–20, 27

Vonnegut, Kurt, 5, 56

West, Nathaniel, 8

Wilde, Oscar, 3

Willingham v. Mason Telegraph Pub. Co., 38, 43–45

Wilson v. Southwest Airlines, 30–31, 42, 60, 70–71

Library of Congress Cataloging-in-Publication Data

Post, Robert.

Prejudicial appearances : the logic of American antidiscrimination law /

Robert C. Post with K. Anthony Appiah . . . [et al.].   p. cm.   Includes index.

ISBN 0-8223-2702-3 (cloth : alk. paper) — ISBN 0-8223-2713-9 (pbk. : alk. paper)

1. Discrimination — Law and legislation — United States. 2. Physical

— appearance-based bias. 3. Prejudices. I. Title.

KF4755 .P67 2002   342.73'087 — dc21   2001033629